God bless you Lisa!

In Christ –
Meg

Romans 8:28

CODE 1

Meg Jordan

WESTBOW
P R E S S
A DIVISION OF THOMAS NELSON

WestBow Press books may be ordered through booksellers or by contacting:

WestBow Press
A Division of Thomas Nelson
1663 Liberty Drive
Bloomington, IN 47403
www.westbowpress.com
1-(866) 928-1240

ISBN: 978-1-4497-8267-2 (sc)
ISBN: 978-1-4497-8266-5 (hc)
ISBN: 978-1-4497-8268-9 (e)

Library of Congress Control Number: 2013901239

Printed in the United States of America

WestBow Press rev. date: 2/1/2013

Table of Contents

Dedication vii

Introduction..ix

Preface xiii

Chapter 1   Wrong Place, Wrong Time? 1

Chapter 2   My Foundation.....................................14

Chapter 3   A Child's Way.......................................20

Chapter 4   Four-Letter Word..................................24

Chapter 5   Dad's Decline 36

Chapter 6   Looking Back to Step Forward 48

Chapter 7   Life in the Surreal World 54

Chapter 8   Judgment Day.......................................65

Chapter 9   The Trial...74

Chapter 10 Fifty-Three Minutes 83

Chapter 11 Adversity Brings Change.......................89

Chapter 12 My New Beginning 94

Chapter 13 Stepping into Step-Motherhood............98

Chapter 14 Tick Tock, It's God's Clock..................104

Chapter 15 GPS 112

Chapter 16 Happy Father's Day 122

Chapter 17 The Next Step...133

Chapter 18 Not Just a Band-Aid 139

Chapter 19 I Have a Brown Thumb 144

Chapter 20 Reflections of the Ascent............................... 151

Chapter 21 The Greatest Love of All 167

Chapter 22 That's Life! 174

Chapter 23 There Is Purpose in Pain 181

Chapter 24 His Work on the Cross 186

Chapter 25 The New You... 190

Chapter 26 Your Elevator Speech 194

Chapter 27 My Father's Wisdom... 198

Acknowledgments 205

References 209

About the Author... 211

Dedication

I dedicate this book in loving memory of my father, Bruce. He was a man who wanted the simple things out of life: happiness, to help others, to laugh until it hurts, and to have a purposeful existence. He was blessed with integrity, sincerity, and endless intellectual capacity. He had a passion for helping people and shared his lessons on life through his stories and catchy phrases, such as "Nobody's perfect," "Do your best," "Stand up for what you believe in," "Take life one day at a time," "Always be yourself," and "Life's not fair." He approached the world from a different yet intriguing way. He was often misunderstood by his peers because he thought about things in the big picture, not focusing on small, unimportant issues. His general philosophies on life were uniquely simple. He reinforced his own beliefs about life, the fact that sometimes we are handed difficult situations and are left to deal with them.

Through his years on the lacrosse field at Johns Hopkins and the quarter century he spent as a Human Resource manager, Dad learned a lot about human emotion, interaction, and thought. He would tell story after story about nothing at all and turn it into a lesson on life. Outspoken and not afraid of debate, Dad supported his teachings on life with real experiences, even using the difficult times in life as an example to make his point. He was the kind of man who made a lasting impression on every life he touched, particularly mine. For most of his life, he tried to find the humor in every situation.

However, as time moved on, tragic events occurred and challenges became daily occurrences. He lost the hope and faith he had once known as a child. He, like many of us, surrendered to the negativity of our world. His dreams of helping and passion for people slowly fizzled out as Dad settled into a "poor me" mentality. Instead of turning to God for help and guidance, he turned away from Him and lived the last years of his life in a place called "self-pity." He used alcohol to get through the day and to fog his mind from thinking about all the wrongs and hurts he experienced. As his mind gave into those thoughts and painful memories, his body lost the resistance to fight.

Before his passing, my mother and I begged him to write a book about the novelties he had taught us. Dad's response was simply, "I will someday."

On January 13, 1996, at the age of fifty-eight, he died having never written that book.

Introduction

This is my someday.

Have you ever heard the expression, "I was at the wrong place at the wrong time"? Sure. We all have. And most of us have a story somewhere on our life's journey that we tell to illustrate this point. But what if our "wrong place, wrong time" was *God's* "right place, right time" for us? What if His plan for our life was to put us exactly in that "wrong place" at the "wrong time" in order for Him to introduce Himself to us, to grab our attention in a way that draws us closer to Him and the plan *He* has for us? What if what we deem to be a problem or trial is the very thing God sees as an opportunity, His opportunity to reveal Himself to us? Something as simple as changing our focus and perspective can be the very tools that reshape the rest of our lives.

When I am asked, "What is your book about?" the simplest response seems to offer the most intrigue. "It's a story about how God took a tragic situation and is using it for good—His good." More specifically, this book encompasses lesson after lesson about how giving up control brought answered prayers, a deepened faith, and a purposeful life.

The catalyst that began this journey into faith occurred more than ten years ago. It was during a crisis moment, a moment that required quick thinking, fast action, and selfless service. This crisis prompted me to question everything, and more importantly, to begin searching for the purpose of my existence; God's purpose, not mine. God has a unique way of making good out of bad. His Word tells us, "You intended to harm me, but God intended it for good to accomplish what is now being done, the saving of many lives" (Genesis 50:20, New International Version). His work is flawless and perfect. That doesn't mean it's free of pain or that it doesn't cause us to wonder, "Why?"

Walking along God's road is very much like walking along a winding path in the middle of a forest: it is sometimes framed with low-lying limbs or thorns that offer painful pricking. If it's a foggy day, it's difficult to see where the path is leading. But when we get a glimpse of a ray of sunlight through the thickness of the forest's skyline, it can be the most encouraging and invigorating sight that causes us to seek more, to take the next step toward the light—His light. Our journey along God's road constantly moves in new directions. It doesn't end with a specific event. It turns, twists, travels high and low. It continues to be challenged, tested, broken, mended, strengthened, and deepened.

When we first started dating, my husband raved to his friends about how smart I was. I clearly had him fooled! He attributed knowledge and wisdom to a book-filled college education. I laughed at the thought, as I had learned at a young age that the most knowledgeable components to learning are through experience, trial and error, and engaging ourselves in an environment that utilizes the information we gather from reading a book. Applying it. Living it.

One of the most teachable experiences I have had involved a tragedy. A death. But little did I know at that time how many lives would be changed by the event. How my life would be *saved*.

Admittedly, when I initially started writing this book in 1999, part of me wanted some kind of public revenge for all the false comments made about me in the news. I spent years feeling like a victim, angry and disgusted with the world, or at least my small corner of the world. I became bitter, untrusting, and empty. I felt like I had lost my purpose in life—*or maybe I was just allowing fear to derail me.* However, after I had truly turned my life over to Jesus Christ at the age of twenty-five and given up my own agendas for revenge, God began to show me *His* plan for writing this book. He would teach me many, many lessons, starting with this one: "Do not take revenge" (Romans 12:19, NIV). He had a purpose for my journey, and I had to step down from my platform of bitterness in order for Him to take center stage in my life and reveal His purpose.

When I did, it slowly became clear that the thoughts and words were coming from God; He is the fuel behind this book. Without Him, this book would still be sitting in draft form, and I in a pit known as "poor me."

I feel blessed to have learned so much from Him at such a

young age. Many people live their entire lives never having really felt the power of His love, which only occurs when we move away from our own self-promoting agendas and truly allow God to take the reins over our lives. He has a plan for each of us. We just have to trust and follow Him.

Please join me as we journey down the path.

Preface

The views, impressions and memories expressed in this book are solely those of the author. While the story is based upon actual events, the names of the parties involved have been changed.

CHAPTER 1

Wrong Place, Wrong Time?

It was my first job out of college. I worked in an inpatient psychiatric hospital in Greensboro, North Carolina. I was a mental health assistant on the second shift. I worked with kids, helping them deal with life and learn how to navigate through it. I had been there since my graduation in May 1997. I was twenty-two years old.

It was March 4, 1998.

When I arrived at work that day, I anticipated the usual routine. Little did I know that at the end of the shift, instead of clocking out, I would be questioned, challenged, and, most of all, changed. I can recall the sequence of events as if they happened yesterday.

It was shortly after 9:30 p.m. The unit was relatively quiet. Most of our younger patients were fast asleep. I stood leaning against the nurses' station, holding my head in one hand and a pen in the other, charting patients' progress. As I recalled the earlier events of the evening with the young patients, I remember feeling overwhelmed by the number of children we had on our unit and their seemingly endless emotional and psychological needs. Many of those kids were hurting and scared. As overwhelming as the mental-health field is, it is also a humbling and awesome feeling to know I could be a small light in their little worlds of darkness. Though it carried a lot of stress, it also made my life seem a little lighter.

It gave me purpose.

The children's unit sat adjacent to the adolescent unit with the only division being locked glass doors. I looked up in thought from writing progress notes for one patient's chart, trying to recall and document the behavior of a particular little girl on our unit. As I looked up, I glanced through the glass doors and saw "Dana", one of the interns working with the teenagers that night, running toward the adolescent unit nurses' station with a panicked look on her face. Her face displayed a different sense of fear than the "normal" fear of being in that environment. Our eyes met, and she signaled me to come to that unit. I remember an unsettled sensation in my gut. It was unusual and more intense from the other crisis situations I had responded to before. I knew something was wrong. Terribly wrong. I could see the terror in her eyes. My right hand dropped the pen as it reached for the panic unlock button on the wall.

I stepped through doors and watched Dana as she grabbed the speaker to the hospital intercom. Her words, combined with the look on her face, hit me with an eerie chill.

"Code one."

She pointed me in the direction of where the adolescent boys were housed. As I ran toward the end of the hall, I recall hearing the most unbelievable disturbance. Something like a wrestling match, only there was nothing playful about the commotion. My feet didn't seem to run fast enough, though they barely hit the floor between steps. It seemed like it was taking an eternity to get to the room, though it was only a matter of yards away. As she called over the hospital intercom a second time, Dana's terror-filled words hit me again. "Code one, adolescent unit!"

When I arrived at the last room on the right at the end of the hall, I went inside only to find several strong men struggling with all their might to contain an irate and uncontrollable sixteen-year-old boy whose physique was nothing short of a man. They looked at me with a fright I had never seen before. It was "Christopher." Belly down on the floor, surrounded by six of my coworkers who were struggling to restrain him, he was bucking, screaming, cussing, and threatening to hurt anyone who crossed him. Fear and shock struck me like a cold, blustery wind. I had been involved in many code-one situations, but this one had a different impression. It was surreal. After a half-second gasp at what I saw, I reacted. I joined their efforts by kneeling on the floor by Christopher's head.

His head flared as his body bucked. The strength he possessed was animalistic. I tried to hold his head still with my bare hands for fear he would slam it on the thinly carpeted floor, or worse, snap his own neck. At that moment, my mind immediately flashed back to the night before.

3

A Preview of Things to Come

On the afternoon of March 3, 1998 I arrived on the children's unit. I took one look at the patient board and was already exhausted. It was an unusually busy time of year for the mental-health profession. It seemed as though the number of patients had skyrocketed. Unfortunately, while the number of patients admitted to the hospital increased, the number of staff hit a plateau. We were stretched thin. This increase in patient care equated to harder work, longer hours to finish documenting patients' progress, and of course, a greater risk of something going terribly wrong.

I could not believe the ratio of twenty-one children to three staff members. We're talking about twenty-one children dealing and coping with depression, anger, fear, and defiant behavior. These children rarely listened to or respected authority. Many were accustomed to acting as they pleased but were now being told how to behave. It was a culture shock for all of us. Some, not all, were hospitalized by the state, not their mom or dad. This was a lot of emotion and dysfunction for three adults to handle. Luckily, the evening progressed relatively smooth on our unit. We managed to get the kids through group therapy sessions, dinner, family visitations and bath time, and then we laid twenty-one children down to sleep. However, the adolescent unit was experiencing some disruption, which would later snowball into an outburst, which required many of us to intervene.

I remember standing on the children's unit hearing, "Code one, adolescent unit" across the hospital intercom. Two of us ran to the unit while the third stayed behind. We stepped onto the adolescent unit and found a large male patient, Christopher, struggling with two of the staff members on the floor.

One of the other male staff members was kneeling beside me, also trying to stabilize Christopher. During the course of the intervention, the patient thrust his body toward the staff member kneeling beside his shoulder. Christopher leaned over in his direction and attempted to bite his hand. Fortunately, my coworker saw him and was able to quickly pull back.

At that point, I yelled, "He's trying to bite," and a towel was brought to me within seconds. I folded the towel once lengthwise, as I had been trained to do, and placed it over his mouth to prevent him from trying to bite again. The struggle continued for a few more seconds before the patient began to show signs of cooperation. Once he displayed a level of calmness that was acceptable to the nurse in charge, he was then put in a "quiet room" to deescalate further. After a few minutes in the quiet room, the patient was counseled by several adolescent unit staff members and nurses. When they reached a level of comfort with his behavior and statements, he was allowed to leave the quiet room and join the rest of the adolescent patients for group therapy. At that point I, and several of the other staff members who responded to the code, returned to our units. The intervention worked as it was designed to: to keep all patients safe by intervening until he could deescalate and safely return to the unit.

Later that night, all was quiet, and the hospital was secure. Though something about that intervention had really triggered a fear inside me—a different level of precaution than the others

I had been involved in since joining the hospital just ten months prior. There was something different about *that* patient. Looking back now, I can see how this was a preview of things to come.

My mind jolted back to this restraint, March 4. The chaos continued. I remembered his previous attempt at biting my co-worker. Based on that knowledge, I reacted to this intervention by grabbing the closest towel, which was actually a bathmat, smaller in size and length than the hospital towels, but made from the same material. Between his head-butting and bucking, I managed to place it over his mouth. I held the ends of it in my hands on each side of his head. However, he continued to fight, thrashing his head and knocking me off balance from my kneeling position and ripping the towel from my grip.

The tension in that room grew. I had never witnessed such a fierce look on any human's face as I saw on his that night. He was angry, irrational, and out of control—a dangerous combination.

The struggle continued. My efforts had never been challenged at this level before. I, along with six grown men who were trained and experienced with this type of intervention, was growing fatigued. Christopher, however, seemed to gain momentum with hostility, anger, and adrenaline. Still lying on the floor, he continued to thrust his body just as a bull would thrust a rider off its back. Christopher threw his head from left to right, forward to backward. The short towel continued to slip from my hands, falling to the floor. "Ellen", the evening shift nurse supervisor, entered the room in response to the code one. She was stationed on the other end of the hospital with the adult patients. It took her longer to respond to the code.

When she walked through the door of the patient's room, I briefly glanced up at her. Instantly, I noticed her stunted entrance and gasp-of-air response at the scene. Fear immediately consumed her face. In a desperate moment, I looked at her and screamed, "I need a longer towel! I can't keep his head stable." My outburst shook her back into response mode. She ran down the hall and returned with a longer towel, replacing the shorter one.

The violent struggle continued. "I'm going to kick your a**," he shouted at anyone who might respond. He was angry. Though he was outnumbered, his might seemed to overpower us.

The sweat poured down the faces of the staff. We were exhausted. We just needed Christopher to calm down. We could not move him into the quiet room until he was still.

"I'm gonna kill you, —" he screamed.

I tried to reason. "Christopher, it's okay, you just need to calm down so we can help you."

"—you!" he wailed.

"Christopher just calm down," I repeated.

He continued to fight against us to release him.

"Christopher, we need you to listen. Just calm down so we can help you." I reasoned.

"Shut up!" he shouted. "I can't breathe. I'm gonna kill you."

"Christopher, if you're screaming, you're breathing. You need to just calm down." I tried reasoning again. I had seen this tactic by patients in the past. Their hands held down, their feet immobilized by hands of two staff members; the only resource for manipulation was words. Both adults and children in restraints essentially "cry wolf." I knew he could breathe. I could hear him breathing during the struggle. I checked and double-checked the towel for positioning. There was never any physical indication that we, that I, was limiting his air flow. He continued to fight, scream, cuss, and threaten. It was horribly physically and emotionally exhausting. Trying to help a person who doesn't want to be helped is beyond draining. But that's what we had to do. It was our job. It was our duty, for his safety and ours. "I'm gonna kill you all!" he screamed again. We continued our reasoning and intervention. We knew this was no match for his anger, but it was what we were trained to do.

Sounds of a deep-seated grunting came from him. His body still bucked. My hands lost their placement and the towel once again fell to the floor. I was growing more scared and frustrated. We just needed him to calm down and be still. His head once again thrust toward his shoulders. I looked at Ellen. She looked at me with disbelief. "I need something longer. I can't hold this towel in place." She left the room and quickly returned. This time she brought a bed sheet. It was placed over his mouth.

A few more seconds passed, though it felt like minutes. Christopher finally appeared to calm down, exhausted from the struggle, as were we.

"Jack", one of my co-workers nurses assisting in the restraint, said, "Christopher, we need to take you to the quiet room. We need you to stay calm."

He said nothing. He had finally worn himself out, I thought.

Jack looked at all of us, "On my count. One. Two. Three." It took the strength of the seven of us to pick him up, supporting his head, back, feet, arms, and waist. We moved quickly, walking in a shuffle mode. The quiet room, though only at the end of a short hallway, felt like miles away from his room. In less than one minute, we entered the bare-walled room and laid him on the bed, stomach down. "Gary" and "Steve", both mental health assistants, began putting the restraints around his feet. He wasn't moving.

"Wait!" I shouted. "He isn't breathing!"

Once again, fear appeared to consume everyone in the room. I immediately checked for a pulse on the side of his neck. Nothing. "Check the pulse in his wrist!" I screamed. Jack and Ellen each grabbed an arm to check for a beat. Nothing. We flipped him onto his back and several of us shouted. "Start CPR!"

Jack began manually compressing Christopher's chest while Ellen reached for the airbag. She furiously pumped air into him, but only his abdomen began to ascend, not his chest. "Move him to the floor! We need a hard surface against his back". I heard someone say. We grabbed each extremity and lifted him off the bed, onto the hard, cold floor.

"Get the crash cart!" Another nurse yelled.

"Call a code blue! Call 9-1-1!" Someone else shouted.

Nurses came out of the woodwork. Everyone's efforts that night were to save Christopher's life. I held the mask over his mouth while "Jennifer", another nurse, pumped the air. Jack continued chest compressions. Our efforts to save him continued for several minutes.

As the adrenaline pumped through our veins, I thought, *this isn't happening. It can't be happening.* Some of the finest nurses I had ever seen were trying to save his life. Their level of skill and effort was apparent. I remember looking down at his face. His eyes were wide open, pupils dilated.

At that moment, my mind flashed back to my father lying in the hospital bed just two years earlier. The blank stare in his eyes and the lifeless body was a vivid reflection of watching my dad as he slipped away from this world. The painful memory, the fear and grief that I felt at that moment was overwhelming. "I can't handle this! Someone take my place."

A nurse stepped in my place to hold the mask. I left the quiet room, went to the nurses' station, and sat on the floor. My hands held my head as the tears hit the floor. *Is this really happening?*

The paramedics showed up only minutes after the code blue and the emergency medical services were called. Though I didn't watch the two EMTs administer care, I listened to the struggle they too faced.

"I can't get the line in. I need a different vein." Moments later they pushed Christopher out on the stretcher while radioing to the closest medical hospital.

I looked up at Christopher. He was white, lifeless. I knew he was gone. My eyes followed the stretcher down the hall. At one point my focus shifted to one of my coworkers. He was kneeling in the hallway, hands clenched.

He was praying.

After the paramedics took Christopher out on the stretcher, I made a call home. I was living, unmarried, with my boyfriend,

"Jim". He answered, heard my shaking voice and instantly knew something was wrong. "I don't know what time I'll be home, but it will be late."

He asked, "What happened?"

I cried and said, "I honestly don't know. I'll see you later." What *had* just happened? I wanted an answer. My head fell into my hands. I cried.

Ellen gathered all of us into a conference room. She knew we were in no condition to go back to our units. We sat around the table, stunned, exhausted bodies, emptied looks, and confused hearts. We were now the ones in need of help. We needed someone to tell us what happened. We needed to understand.

Shortly after the paramedics left, detectives arrived at the hospital, some wearing police uniforms, some not. They entered the room, and the lead detective spoke. "We're here to help figure out what happened. We're not looking to blame anyone, and we won't be taking anyone to jail … yet."

I looked up at him. He had a smug look on his face.

Was that supposed to be funny?

He continued. "We have several officers here who will talk to each of you individually. Please do not discuss this among yourselves; wait until you are called to see a detective." I should have tuned into that mentality right there. But my mind was so clouded with disbelief about this death that I couldn't rationalize that one, or all of us, might actually be accused of causing this terrible tragedy—even though the *only* thing any of us wanted to do was to help, to *prevent* him from getting hurt.

Our choice of profession was not made based on monetary gain. We weren't handed the keys to company cars. In fact, many evening-shift workers were left without a break for dinner. We were all there to help. We wanted to make a positive difference in the lives of the patients who crossed our path. I wanted to make at least one child's life easier and brighter. I never imagined this motivation and desire to help could lead to an indictment.

Jack stood up from his chair and said, "I think we need to have an attorney present before we speak to these detectives."

My faced exhibited disbelief. He was thinking clearly, despite an unclear event. *I don't need an attorney—I didn't do anything wrong,* I thought. I wanted to give them as much information as possible so they could figure out this mysterious and unexplained death.

At that point, we got the word from the detectives: Christopher was pronounced dead at the hospital. "Susan Ritter", one of the hospital's administrators, had been called in. It was now close to 11 p.m. Susan was asked to contact "Mary Jones", the hospital's attorney.

They told us it would be in our best interest to have Mary present at all interviews with the police. I agreed. I just wanted to give the police my account of what had transpired so I could go home. I was physically and mentally empty. I just needed to cry in the privacy of my own home. We each waited, for hours, to speak to the detectives.

When I finally spoke with the detective, I told him about the details of the night. I recalled what I saw and what I did. My role. My actions. My intentions. I told him about Christopher's threat to hurt himself, and his unwillingness to cooperate with the staff, which prompted the intervention. I articulated how hostile he was, out of control, and full of rage. He asked me about the towel. I relayed the struggle and the use of the bed sheet. His responses never led me to believe he suspected I had done anything wrong. I relayed Christopher's verbal threats. I recalled the specific details about the restraint from the previous night, with the indication of biting and the reasoning for the use of the towel.

The detective sat in his chair, unmoved by my account. We concluded the interview, and I returned to the conference room. The night was over.

I looked at Ellen and asked, "Can I take tomorrow off? I don't think I can handle this right now."

"No," she responded. "We can't afford you to take off. None of us can. This consumed the entire staff tonight. I'm sorry."

The drive home was long. Though totally exhausted, my eyes were wide open, like those of a deer in headlights. I replayed the night over and over during the twenty-five-minute drive. I stepped through the back door at 4:32 a.m. Jim was asleep. I went in and lay beside him. He rolled over and put his arm around me. I flooded our bed with tears. He didn't say anything. He just held me. That was all I needed at that moment.

I couldn't recount it again in full detail. "We restrained an adolescent patient tonight. He died." I sobbed. "I don't know what went wrong, but he died."

CHAPTER 2

My Foundation

Mom is the oldest of five kids, four girls and one boy. They lived in the South and followed the religious mold of the region: church on Wednesday nights, Sunday morning, and Sunday nights. She sang in the choir with her sisters. She was raised to be loving, caring, patient, proper, and Godly. Shortly after graduating high school she left home and headed to New Orleans with her sister Jean. She applied and was accepted into school to be a flight attendant. She loved to travel and quickly found a passion serving others across the friendly skies. She is a caregiver—whether on a plane, in a PTA meeting, or watching her grandchildren during a parents' night out—Mom's passion is caring for others.

Dad was raised in Maryland as a single child. His parents were structured, and proper. As a child, he was forced to attend church on Sunday morning. After all, it was the proper thing to do. His German mother was a strong-willed and stubborn-minded woman who said what she felt and didn't concern herself with who might take offense. Dad graduated from Johns Hopkins University with a degree in engineering, though he often reiterated how much he despised the pressure his parents put on him to get that degree. His passion was people.

And lacrosse.

He played lacrosse for Hopkins and was an all-American star for four years. Whether he was in the classroom or on the lacrosse field, he was analytical and observant of other people's behavior. Following graduation, Dad accepted a job as a Human Resource manager for a major international telephone service provider corporation. He was more than just a manager. He was a teacher and a leader and was idolized by many people. His understanding of humans was phenomenal. He could understand feelings and thoughts better than any psychologist I have ever encountered. Shortly after his employment began, he married his first wife, Judy, and later had two daughters Amy and Lisa. His glory of being a father was stricken with tragedy when his older daughter, Amy, died at the age of three. Riddled with unbelievable pain, confusion, and guilt, Dad's marriage began to crumble. He was divorced shortly after. He began questioning God and turned to vodka to deal with the grief.

Dad's relationship with God was never the same.

They met on a plane. Mom was accustomed to businessmen flirting with her during long flights across the country. Although she dismissed most of the passengers' flirtatious behavior, she says,

"Your dad was different." They caught each other's eye, and he asked if he could call her sometime.

Two years later, on Valentine's Day, they married.

My brother, Jason, was born May 31, 1971, and I was born on May 20, 1975. Growing up in a suburban part of New Jersey, we had the ideal life. My father earned a good living. After my brother was born, Mom quit her job as a flight attendant and was able to be a stay-at-home mom. I hold a great amount of respect for her. Unlike most working adults who go to one job each day, Mom had *several* careers. She was a chef, a nurse, a chauffeur, a maid, and a teacher. She fed us, cleaned us, taught us, loved us, and gave us freedom to explore life and pursue our passions. I am grateful to my parents for providing for, caring for, and loving me in the manner they did. Mom and Dad were firm believers that experience is the best way to learn, grow, and mature.

They let us take risks and learn from our experiences. Like a toddler taking his or her first steps, my parents realized that in order for us to learn and grow, we had to fall down in the process. There's an old saying: "When you're at the bottom of your barrel, the only way to go is up." Mom and Dad let us do just that—they would allow us to fall down but always stood nearby to pick us back up.

In addition to the love and nurturing home they provided, our parents taught us more through observing their morals and principles. During my childhood, I experienced positive and negative times, as any child does. Dad preached, on more than one occasion, about how "the world is an unfair place." Many times, we "are just in the wrong place at the wrong time." Both lessons would later seem to hold true during the course of my young life.

The best word I can find to describe my childhood is naïve. I was naïve in believing the world is a wonderful place and that all the people in the world are good, with good intentions and no hidden agendas. I was also naïve to go through life believing a person would never be held accountable for something he or she did not do or did not cause to happen. My parents are wonderful people who taught me many things, but sometimes I feel like I may have been too sheltered as a child. Or perhaps I just got hit hard as a young adult, after been treated so well as a young child.

My dad and I had a special connection, one every father and daughter should have. Not only was I "Daddy's little girl," I also tended to follow in his footsteps and still do today, in many respects. I was always fascinated to hear him speak about his experiences in college and work.

I remember one story Dad shared with me before I went to college. He told me about a philosophy class he had taken. It was the time of year most college students dread, final exams. After many hours of preparation for this particular exam, Dad said he walked into the classroom and took his seat for the three-hour test. It consisted of one very difficult question: "Why?"

The professor wrote this word on the chalkboard and left the room. For the next three hours, the class sat and wrote and wrote and wrote. They created their individual soul-searching, mind-boggling, and earth-shattering responses. When the exam concluded, the professor returned. He asked the class to stop writing and put down their pens.

He approached the chalk board and wrote the answer: "Why not?"

The class had completely missed the lesson. Dad said everyone had missed the entire meaning. The answer was simple, so basic, yet so many had tried to make it difficult.

We are all like that at times. We take something so easy to understand and twist and turn it until we not only don't have an answer but answer it with more questions.

There were many times Dad amazed me with his knowledge and experiences. I hated to play board games, particularly Trivial Pursuit, with him but loved it at the same time. It was fun, yet frustrating. While I struggled to search my limited knowledge for answers to the questions, Dad never broke a sweat answering his. I could not understand how one person could retain so much information—albeit trivial and useless. But still, to have the knowledge and memory that he possessed were *gifts*.

Dad and I also shared a common bond through sports. I played soccer and softball in high school. He taught me more about the game, the strategy, than I ever learned from my coaches. He taught me to think, anticipate, and react. His often said to me, "When in doubt, go." In other words, if you hesitate to ponder and overanalyze the situation, you lose time and opportunity.

I was a goalkeeper in soccer, so that advice constantly played in my head. I vividly remember one moment of one game in particular. We were playing our biggest rival. The score was 0-0. It was close to the end of the game. The striker from the opposing team had weaved her way through our defensive line, and the only person stopping her from scoring was me. I was the last person standing in the way of their victory. I could stand still, *frozen in fear*, on the goal line and wait for the striker's approach, giving her a wide, open goal to aim for. Or I could *step* forward, face the opposition, and minimize the angle of her target. The pressure and anticipation grew inside me, and I could hear my own heart beating, silencing the roar of the spectators. I started to doubt my abilities. I didn't know what to do; I just knew I had to do *something*.

I had to act.

I immediately resorted to Dad's logic: "When in doubt, go." I could hear the voice from inside. I bolted toward her as she continued to approach me; she fired her shot as I dove to block the ball. As my hands hit the ball, my body hit the ground. I had thought, anticipated, and acted, just as Dad had told me to. It worked. She didn't score, and I had become a hero to Dad. Not because I had prevented the goal but because I acted on instinct with confidence in my decision. I remember this overwhelming feeling of satisfaction. I had taken Dad's advice, and my entire team benefited. I don't recall if we won the game or not, but that really didn't have an effect on how I felt. I was proud, win or lose. *I followed my father's advice, took a step forward, and chose not to let doubt and fear paralyze me.*

CHAPTER 3

A Child's Way

I love children. My first babysitting job was at the age of twelve for a family of five that lived down the street. Sally and Jeff had just relocated to the area and were the parents of three young children. They met in college. Jeff stood more than six feet tall, had blue eyes, and was strong from years of collegiate swimming. Sally stood slightly less than five feet, had blonde hair, blue eyes, and was cute. They were quite a pair and their love for one another, as well as the love they had for their three children, was displayed all over their faces. They had one daughter, age four and two boys, ages two and one. Like any good parent, they were a little apprehensive about leaving their children with a new person, especially one who was only twelve.

The first time I watched the kids I fell instantly in love with them. Sarah was blonde-haired, blue-eyed, and brilliant. She loved to read, even at the young age of four. Two-year-old Tommy was just learning to climb and get into little boy trouble. He had a sense of humor and a laughter that would drown out the noise in the Rose Bowl Stadium. Scotty, still in diapers, was just learning to walk. He tumbled like the best of them and giggled along the way. They were adorable beyond belief, full of energy and heartwarming to be around. A seed of loving children had been planted in me through this family.

Over the course of several years, I babysat these kids on countless occasions. I never looked at it as a job. Watching these kids grow, become excited about learning to read, and take their first steps in life was magical. It was more of an honor to witness than a job.

We grew close. One summer during my high-school days, they took a family vacation with another family of five kids. That family had hired a babysitter to accompany them to the beach for a week. Excited about the idea of having a "true adult night" at the beach, Sally and Jeff asked if I would to spend the week with their family too. I happily agreed.

We packed up the cars. Yes. Cars, plural. Another life lesson learned early—having kids means packing the up the house! We were all packed and headed to the Jersey shore. I witnessed the enthusiasm of kids as they experienced a huge ocean with lots of sand to dig in! The week was laid back, full of fun in the sun and laughter. Sarah, now nine, was aggressive in her own way. She swam furiously in the ocean and "rode" the waves. Tommy, a little more reserved though still adventurous, tackled the ocean too. Jeff and I stood at the edge of the water while Scotty played in the sand.

The tides had gotten more intense as the week progressed. A riptide had set in and we suddenly watched Sarah and Tommy struggle to get back onto the shoreline. Jeff plunged into the water and swam with all his might. I felt a strong instinct to follow but stayed back to watch and care for the littlest child. The other babysitter plunged in after Jeff. They both grabbed a child and fought the current back to the beach. I felt a surge of emotions: horror knowing that in only an instant, life could have taken a terrible turn, and adrenaline flooded my body in response to the imminent danger. And, ironically, I most vividly remember a feeling of frustration. I couldn't run in after the children swept out by the current because I had to watch the youngest and keep him safe. There was a *need for help* ... and circumstances didn't allow me to respond. It was an interesting inner psychological struggle, and one I would later learn is called the "fight or flight" syndrome.

Dr. Neil Neimark states, "The 'fight or flight response' is our body's primitive, automatic, inborn response that prepares the body to 'fight' or 'flee' from perceived attack, harm, or threat to our survival" (Neimark, 2012). Simply put, the fight-or-flight response refers to one of two ways people will respond in an emergency or to an eminent danger. They will either, run to it and offer help, "the fight", or they will run from it and seek safety, "the flight." Neither way is bad or wrong; it's just how we are wired to respond.

I am a fighter. I am compelled to run toward threatening situations and help in whatever way I can. When circumstances prevent me from responding, I experience an inner struggle, one that feels limiting and leaves me frustrated.

The week at the beach went on with many more laughs and good times. Everyone had a great time and came home with a great tan. I also came home with memories that have played over in my head so many times. Those children taught me so much about life, about how we need to laugh a little more and just how precious life really is. Those children, that trip, and that moment of danger helped me recognize and define my passion; I wanted to help others.

CHAPTER 4

Four-Letter Word

Dad loved doing crossword puzzles. He was a quick thinker and could knock them out in minutes. Each day he spent time solving the crossword puzzle in our daily newspaper. One clue in particular, reoccurred several times in different versions of the newspaper.

"Four letters, small private college in southeast."

As the end of my senior year was approaching, I began thinking about life after high school. As I explored my avenues, I realized college was the next chapter in my book of life. Through my journey of researching schools, I discovered a wonderful "small private college in southeast," Elon. I remember the day Dad and I visited Elon College. We had been in other parts of North Carolina visiting other schools. I placed a call to the admissions office at Elon and told them we would be stopping by "at some point during the day."

Several hours later, unannounced, we arrived at the campus on a brisk morning in March. Despite the fact that it was early March and a very cool morning, the campus was absolutely gorgeous. The campus boasted brick buildings. Deep emerald-green grass, plants, and flowers lined the brick walkways. It was like walking through a well-kept golf course—only much, much better.

On the main part of the campus was a breathtaking fountain with cascading waters that drowns out any thoughts. The fountain stood near the beautiful brick Powell building covered in ivy, which housed the admissions office. We walked into the admissions office, without having said a word to anyone.

The receptionist looked at me and said, "Hello, Megan."

I looked at her and said, "How did you know my name is Megan?"

Her response was simple. "We've been expecting you."

While I was given the guided tour, the admissions ambassador continued to tell me about Elon, its commitment to service, its small, quaint community feeling, and the *engaged learning* approach to education. Within minutes of leaving the steps of the admissions office, I knew I would shortly be calling Elon home. At that point, the beautiful landscaping, tall brick buildings covered in ivy, and cascading water fountains didn't seem as important.

"We've been expecting you." Those few words mattered. I felt at home. The receptionist made me feel like I was a person, not a number.

It was ironic that Dad and I visited Elon College together because of the nature and belief of the school. Elon is a school that focuses much of its attention on engaged learning, experience outside the classroom. Trial and error. For years, Dad always preached about getting out there and trying new things. "You'll never know until you try." Plus, Elon's focus on community service, helping others, was right up my alley and something we shared as well. Dad was the type of person who would do anything for anyone, despite any personal cost.

I loved that about him.

The next August, fall 1993, I enrolled at Elon. Mom, Dad, and I packed up my things and once again ventured out on the long nine-hour trip to Elon. After we arrived at my tiny dorm room and unloaded all my stuff, it was time to say good-bye. I remember vividly as the three of us cried together, Dad held me in his arms and with a shaky voice said, "This is your home now." I have never seen the look in his Caribbean-blue eyes like I remember them looking that day. It was a look of pride, love, and sadness. He was proud of my effort, loved me for being true to myself, and sad for our day of departure.

I knew from day one I wanted to study psychology. I had always enjoyed helping people, listening, and, truth be told, giving advice. After having lived with the dysfunctional issues associated with an alcoholic parent and dealing with teenage life in general, I dreamed about working with teens as a guidance counselor in a high school who faced these and other types of family issues.

Despite my excitement about starting school, my first year was rough, to say the least. I couldn't stop thinking about what I had left behind. I was plagued with home-sickness, fear, and an overall sense of uneasiness. I talked to my parents every day, at least once. I missed them terribly. We cried together. My family was very close. I shared every problem, detail, and thought with them and *usually* looked forward to their feedback. Dad had a habit of saying "life's not fair" or "nobody's perfect." He always seemed to have some cliché for me.

My mom tells me there were so many times she wanted to get in the car, drive to Elon and bring me home. She knew that wasn't the answer. I would later learn in life that *being uncomfortable isn't always a bad place to be.* It makes you appreciate where you've been and stirs a desire to search for a new place to go—*to find that comfort and peace you once knew.*

During my sophomore year, I was presented with the opportunity of a lifetime.

Spring break was quickly approaching. Many students were planning to spend their week lying on a beach, drowning in tequila. A friend of mine had scheduled a different agenda. She was part of a group on campus that spent hours helping people rebuild their lives while constructing adequate housing. She knew I didn't have plans for the break and asked me to join a group going to Georgia to build a house for a family in need of basic amenities—running water, electricity, and a house with unbroken windows.

I must admit I was skeptical about spending a week in a remote part of southern Georgia, doing hard labor instead of heading home to see my family or spending it lying on a beach, as most of my peers had planned. I thought about it more and more and finally decided to give it a try; of course my friends had to go with me. During a pre-trip planning meeting, we met the rest of the crew who were also spending their spring break with us in Americus, a small town in Georgia, where the purpose of helping others permeated the entire community.

As other students packed their cars with sunscreen, beach towels, and anticipation of relaxing sunsets, we prepared our bags with hammers, work boots, and a willing heart. We met in the student parking lot at six a.m. and piled into the van. For the next eight hours, I talked with the other students. During the long journey we quickly grew close; it's hard not to when you share such a small space for eight hours! We talked about stuff that was important and not so important. We laughed. We slept. After all, it *was* our spring break. And finally, we arrived at the volunteer house in Americus: the *Amigo House.*

The Amigo House was a place set up for out-of-town volunteers to stay while they work with Habitat for Humanity. It consisted of a kitchen, one bathroom, a living room, and two bedrooms stacked high with bunk beds. Not exactly the Hilton. But with its small and peaceful feeling, this house made me feel like I was in paradise—granted a different sort of paradise from a sand and sun setting.

Monday morning, the alarm went off at six a.m., and I have never wanted to stay in bed more than I did that day. We were exhausted from the ride, and getting up to do hard labor just didn't seem appealing. After hitting the snooze bar several times, we rolled out of bed and threw on some clothes. That was the extent of our primping. Once again we climbed into the van and headed to the work site. The leaders had told us that we would be "building a house in a week."

A house in a week? Yeah right, I thought.

We arrived at the work site. The concrete foundation sat in the middle of a wooded lot. Nothing more. At that point I realized our leaders were not exaggerating when they said we were going to build a house from the ground up! Now, I had swung a hammer in my life, once or twice, hanging up pictures or building a tree fort with my brother. But a house ... where people were actually going to *live?* Reality hit pretty quick. After the first day of sweat, blistered hands, and aches in body parts I didn't even know I had, I was ready to take on more. It is the most unbelievable feeling to help someone else, especially when you have to use your own hands and endure hard labor to do so.

Through the course of the next five days, we met many people while we built this home. One man in particular will always hold a spot in my memory bank. Picture a man, six feet plus, long hair, a hairy face that revealed only his eyes and part of his lips. Scary? Maybe at first, but he soon became one of the most interesting people I had ever met. His name was Walter. He was the construction leader. He taught us how to swing a hammer, hang sheetrock, and roof a house. Of course, *we* provided comic relief with our lack of expertise and skill. He laughed with us and at us. After all, we were just a bunch of college kids with hammers!

But, the people who really made the trip worth all our efforts were the homeowners. The amazed and proud look they had in their eyes when they witnessed the walls of their house go up, the roof that covered those walls, and opening the windows to their new home was beyond words. Imagine, if you can, living in a one-bedroom house, with your spouse and three kids, full of water from leaks, and cold because you couldn't afford new pipes or heating. We were in the business of rebuilding this family's *life*, not just a house. If you've never experienced true poverty like this, be grateful. There are so many people in the world who live in conditions such as these, or worse. It really sickened me to think of the astronomical numbers of families that go without power, heat, and running water. However, the positive component to this scenario is that there *are* people in the world who want to change this, and they are doing it with the help and guidance of Habitat for Humanity. Throughout the week, I repeatedly heard Walter say, "These people are all God's people."

The fact that I was part of this week's adventure was no coincidence. Though I didn't realize it then, each of us was placed there for a reason. This experience was not just about hammers; it was about shaping us into the people we were created to be. I learned more about human emotion and selfless service by giving of my time and energy in that one week than I did during the entire semester in classrooms—that's what I call "engaged learning."

During our time in Americus, we were introduced to Millard Fuller, the founder and president of Habitat for Humanity. We shook his hand and listened to him speak about his experience. I later read more in his book, *The Theology of the Hammer*. He and his wife, Linda, tell their story of how Habitat for Humanity came into existence. They were wealthy, beyond most of our dreams. But as their marriage began to crumble and they were plagued with a feeling of wanting more—not cars, money, or possessions but more substance and meaning in their lives—they turned their futures over to God's direction. They wanted something *real*, something that would give them a sense of true fulfillment. It's what I like to call the "it" factor. It's the sweet spot where your passion intersects with a plan to pursue something meaningful, and something that goes beyond selfish ambition. It stirs a purpose and vision in each of us that some may identify as "your calling" in life.

The Fullers decided to take a step in faith—to surrender their lives to God's plan and to help others. They started Habitat for Humanity. This organization dedicates itself to helping people in need through God's love. The "theology of the hammer is that our Christian faith (indeed, our entire Judeo-Christian tradition) mandates that we do more than just talk about faith and sing about love. We must put faith and love into action to make them real, to make them come alive for people" (Fuller, 7).

At the close of each day, our crew returned to the Amigo House, and we shared our thoughts and feelings. We were grateful for the experience but saddened that our help and the help of others were so desperately needed. At the end of the week after building a new house, establishing new friendships, and reviving hope for the future, we packed up, shed many tears, and were on our way back to school. When we drove back onto campus, we shared with each other some of the feelings we were experiencing. I felt somewhat depressed. I knew there were so many others in the world that would benefit from an experience like this if they would only allow themselves the chance. Although this made me sad for others, I was grateful for the memories and lessons I had acquired in only a week.

I remember what someone said as we were pulling into the parking lot on campus. The experience we had on our spring break trip was like going back to school after Christmas and hearing about all of the presents your friends received and knowing that the *gift* we had just received was so much better, better than anything that could be bought in a store. There is no match to witnessing a look of relief and gratitude on someone's face who genuinely needed help.

No, we didn't have tans. No, we didn't have stories about how much alcohol we consumed (none, to be exact). And no, we didn't have pictures of some tropical island with beautiful sunsets. We had something much more. We had lasting memories built on friendship based on trust and hope for the future. We knew that by helping a family, we'd experienced something better than a great vacation. We had peace of mind that the world has good people who offer good things. It was another affirmation that I wanted to help people for the rest of my life.

After the trip, I began going to Elon's weekly campus chapter meetings of Habitat for Humanity. Much to my surprise, I was nominated and honored with the title of project coordinator for the Elon College campus chapter of Habitat for Humanity. I gladly accepted this new role. I was in charge of coordinating volunteers to work on Saturday mornings with the local county chapter, building houses in our community for people in need. I witnessed other students learn about service, become selfless leaders, and see how the impact of one couples' decision to follow God's direction in their life is changing the world, one nail at a time. It's interesting, actually. During the entire week I spent helping that family in Georgia, I no longer felt homesick. It gave me perspective, a new way of looking at life.

Passion. Vision. Purpose. *Those nails helped me define mine.*

In addition to my involvement with Habitat during my college years, I also worked part time at Elon Homes for Children, a group home for troubled children. Many of the children had been brought there because the circumstances at the homes were unsafe, neglectful, and not conducive to creating productive lives. Some of the older kids had been placed in the group home following poor choices that led to legal issues, requiring the state to intervene.

My position required me to work weekends and sometimes at night, whenever I could schedule times around my classes. My first shift was definitely an eye-opening experience. I was escorting a group of girls, in their early teens, from one building on the campus to the chapel. Several of the children were part of the Christmas play, and they had rehearsal that evening. After a few chords of the first song, a fight broke out between two of the teen boys.

One of the girls suddenly made a dash for the front door of the chapel. Not having any experience with a crisis like this before, my heart skipped a beat. Faced with a dilemma, much like the one I faced with the children at the beach many years prior, I quickly made the decision to follow her, which meant I had to leave the other girls behind, hoping they would not take advantage of the situation. I finally caught up with the hysterical teen girl. I knew very little about her, as this was my first night on the job.

I asked her what was wrong. "Why did you run out of the chapel?"

She told me, between deep breaths, that the boys who had started the fight were her boyfriend and her brother. To this day, I don't really understand the reasoning for the disagreement. I just focused on the fact that this young person was so upset and needed something; I just didn't know what. I could not comprehend why she made such a scene. And then it hit me— maybe she just wanted someone, anyone, to notice her and give her some attention. We all need attention from time to time, but I had never experienced a cry for it, like the way this girl cried. I wrapped my arms around her and guided her back to the chapel to reunite with the other kids. I felt good about what I had done. *I reacted and met a need.* I had helped her, and I loved the way that made me feel.

I had a purpose for being there that night; maybe more than one.

At the conclusion of my shift, the supervisor commended me on my effort and decisiveness in a crisis situation. I still felt like I had not done anything that changed the life for that child. I just simply met a need. She needed someone to care for her. Who knows if she was changed from my action? I hope so. I know I was. This feeling—the soulful feeling of knowing something I did or said changed someone's life for the better, even if for a moment—was invigorating. I felt alive. I felt purposeful. And I wanted more of it. The days I spent at Elon, working with Habitat and the children in the group home, showed me the importance of another four-letter word: help. Helping others helped me discover my passion, vision, and purpose in life.

CHAPTER 5

Dad's Decline

Following my spring break trip, the end of the semester quickly approached. At the end of my sophomore year, I returned home to New Jersey. That summer my father's health began to decline. He had been a diabetic for more than twenty years and his kidneys were failing. Diabetes mixed with gallons of vodka and orange juice, over several years, were a lethal combination for kidneys. My parents waited to tell me until I came home. They were concerned this news would have a negative effect on my emotional state and would interfere with my exams and final papers. When they finally did share this news, I was obviously upset. But part of me had expected this. My dad was a wonderful man, father, and teacher. However, just as the rest of us, he had his weaknesses. He turned to alcohol to cope with life's troubles. He chose this route as a way out from his emotions.

Unfortunately, he was unable to see or admit that the alcohol was adding to the already-difficult equation of depression and anxiety. As his health began to fail, my parents decided moving closer to my mother's family in Florida would be a good solution to his health problems. Mom would have help and support on the difficult road ahead. We packed up, said our good-byes to lifelong friends, and headed south. Considering everything, I felt as though I needed an out too.

I was anxious to go back to school. August quickly approached, and I returned to Elon. My junior year started off with a bang. I was again nominated for the position of project coordinator at Habitat. Our campus chapter had taken on a new challenge and set a goal of raising the funds to finance and build one house per year. We were fired up to reach it! This may not seem significant, but when you think about the typical lives of college students with hectic schedules and heavy class loads, this was a big commitment and goal.

To help us accomplish this task, we were supported by the local county chapter of Habitat. I was so inspired by my trip that I wanted to give others a similar experience each Saturday, weather permitting. Habitat to me was much more than building; it was inspiring, it was uplifting, and it was good old-fashioned hard work that left me with a feeling of accomplishment and purpose. When you spend time with others less fortunate than yourself, you begin to show gratitude for things you had previously taken for granted. I began to see real changes in my attitude. I complained less. I thanked more. And I focused on the needs of others more than mine.

We worked with other leaders to raise money and awareness

about poverty. We devoted hours to spread the mission of Millard Fuller, "Building houses in God's love with people in need." It is the love of helping others that I hold within me that keeps me pushing forward in good times and bad. Through the generosity of others, we were able to obtain land to begin the building process. Our chapter was bigger than ever, both through numbers and spirit and the eagerness to help others was growing rapidly. I was amazed and excited about the amount of people who had heard the three magic words: "Habitat for Humanity," and were coming to each weekly chapter meeting to find out what was behind this mission.

In no time at all, the foundation of the house was complete, and the funds were rolling in like we never could have imagined. I was up each Saturday morning ready to put in our few hours of hard work. The volunteers were eager to learn how to swing a hammer while standing beside the people who would later call this house "home." This was going to be the best year of college yet! The fall was coming to a close and the weekends were becoming scarce due to inclement weather. However, we found other ways to keep the spirits high. I organized a Habitat retreat.

We went to a local park and played games with the focus on building trust among the team members. We tackled ropes courses and "challenge walls". These are physical activities designed to foster group work by depending on teammates in order to be successful in completing the challenge; climbing over a very high wall while only utilizing each other's physical strength. After completing these challenges, we spent time reflecting on the work we had accomplished thus far. It was an effective way to keep the team spirit alive during the times when we were unable to build. Reflection was an integral part of the team-building process; without it, the events were nothing more than games.

As the fall came to a close, Thanksgiving was right around the corner. I had planned to fly home and be with my family. My flight was set; it was just a matter of time until we would be together. I remember waking up one morning to a phone call. On the other end of the line I heard my mother's shaking voice. She was calling to tell me my father had been taken to the emergency room that morning. He experienced shortness of breath. When he had tried to stand and get out of bed, he fell.

After several tests, it was confirmed: Dad had a heart attack. It's ironic, but he was lucky in one sense. After the doctors took a closer look, they discovered three of his arteries were ninety percent blocked. It was a miracle he had not died. The doctors did not want to wait any longer before doing a triple bypass surgery.

The next day, I was on a flight home to see Dad after his surgery. When I walked into his intensive care room, I was overwhelmed by fear. Mom and Jason had tried to warn me about the number of tubes, wires, and machines he was hooked up to, but there's no way to adequately prepare someone before seeing a loved one in this condition. In fact, my body responded to this frightful sight by passing out in the ICU. I woke up as my brother carried me to a couch in the hallway while a nurse fed me orange juice. I had never passed out before, nor had I ever seen my dad in this critical condition.

The next few days were the most crucial. To my surprise, the expectation of heart patients following surgery is to get up and begin walking soon after heart surgery to prevent fluids from building up. However, my dad was facing two battles—recovering from surgery and struggling with the loss of his kidney function. The drinking had finally taken its toll on his body, and it was slowly shutting down. He was unable to get up and walk as soon as the doctors had hoped. The excess buildup of fluid in his lungs led to pneumonia, making breathing nearly impossible.

More than one week after his surgery, Dad was moved out of ICU onto the cardiology floor. He still had not been able to walk, and his strength lessened with each passing day. Just two days after his transfer from units, a nurse called Mom, Jason, and I at two a.m. to tell us Dad had gone into respiratory arrest and they'd had to intubate him to help him breathe. Our feet hit the floor and the clothes hit our back.

We were wide awake and rushing to be with Dad. The drive felt like a journey across country. By the time we arrived, he had been moved back into ICU. Once we got there we did everything humanly possible to keep his spirits up and convince him to keep fighting to stay alive. I look back now and realize our fight for his life was more than just a fight for him. It was battle for one more day, one more week. We were not ready to let him go, regardless of his body's agenda.

As a young woman, the thoughts of my father walking me down the aisle or holding my firstborn were the adrenaline sparks I needed to keep pushing forward and holding on to him. After several days of constant care from the doctors and nurses, Dad's condition stabilized. Although still unable to communicate or walk, he was alive.

As the weekend came to an end, I was faced with the reality that I had to go back to school and take my final exams. I asked Dad to keep fighting and reassured him I would be with him in heart and spirit and would be with him again in a short amount of time.

When I got back to Elon, I was upset and angry. I was upset I had to go on with my life at school, which now seemed so insignificant in the bigger picture. I cannot tell you how I managed to sit through exams and read some meaningless questions while my father lay in a hospital room fighting to breathe. I kept trying to tell myself I had to take these exams for Dad. He was going to be okay and would be upset if I had let my schoolwork slip. I turned in my paper and headed back to my dorm, not to study for the next exam but to call home for a status.

Mom told me his condition had not changed, and neither had his demeanor. She reassured me returning to school was the right thing to do. She said, "Daddy will be okay, and he is very proud of you."

That seemed to help, but I felt guilty for returning to school and not being home with my family during this crisis. I was angry and found myself in a similar place that Dad had been after his three-year-old daughter died.

Thoughts rushed through my mind. After experiencing the goodness of God on the Habitat trip, this situation caused me to question. *If there really is a God, why is He punishing Dad through this suffering?* Dad had finally come to a realization that his drinking was hurting him—killing him—and he realized he needed help. *And now,* I thought, *God won't heal him?* Did Dad really deserve this? Did any of us deserve this type of treatment and suffering? It all seemed so inhumane and certainly lacking mercy and compassion. *Why won't God heal him and make this go illness go away?* I simply did not understand.

I was also angry with Dad. (It has taken a lot of time, counseling, soul searching, and tissues to be able to admit I was mad at my dad.) My anger toward him was simple. *How could he do this to himself, and to us?* All the years of drinking, smoking, and unhealed hurt had finally caught up with him. He could have chosen to take care of himself, but he didn't. And now, because of his choices, we had to deal with an enormous amount of pain and worry.

If God really loves us the way He claims to, then why was this happening?

After my exams were finished, I packed my things for my trip to Florida for Christmas. I heard friends talking about the new CD player, TV, or car they wanted for Christmas. All I wanted was my dad alive and healthy again. I yearned for him to sit up in that hospital bed and say, "Hey, Shorty," as he had done so many times during my childhood.

The reality was, I knew that time away from school would be spent in a hospital room, watching Dad suffer and slowly deteriorate, not exactly my picture of the perfect Christmas or one to be thankful for. As Mom, Jason, and I spent long hours watching over and talking to Dad, the days seemed to creep by. We left to go home the night before Christmas to catch some rest before we returned to the hospital. We didn't say much to each other on our drive home. Following a solemn gift exchange Christmas morning (a weak attempt at feeling happy), we quickly said our thanks, ate some breakfast, and were on our way back to the hospital. It was difficult to be festive knowing the odds were stacked against Dad for a full recovery. The thought of losing him was the most painful emotion I had ever experienced. The only thing we wanted was not found under the tree wrapped in shiny paper.

We were greeted by the nurses and shortly thereafter received the best present anyone could have asked for. Dad had come off the ventilator and was breathing on his own! We all burst into tears of joy. We spent the rest of the day reading Christmas cards to Dad from family and friends. I look back now and see that a lot of what we did and what we said to him was for our benefit more than his. Though off the ventilator, Dad was still oblivious to what was going on around him and still too weak to speak. I guess we tried to fill in the blanks with insignificant topics, anything to break the silence and sounds of all the medical machines.

Soon after Christmas, the doctors approached us to say they felt Dad had reached a point in his recovery that a rehabilitation hospital was where he needed to be. Mom, Jason, and I were shocked by this simply because Dad was still so lifeless and unable to get out of bed that we just could not imagine him in a hospital setting that would demand this type of exertion from his weak body. We spoke to the doctors and presented our concerns. They reassured us this was the next step he needed in order to reach a point of becoming independent of machines. So we put our trust in the doctors and took their advice.

As the new year chimed in, it was time for me to return to Elon for the winter semester. I wrestled with staying home, given Dad's medical state, but Mom assured me he would want me to go back to school. A few days after my departure, Dad was transferred to a rehabilitation hospital in northern Florida. Jason and Mom drove three hours every day to see him. I called daily to get reports on his progress; my focus was clearly not on my studies.

At first he seemed to be doing well, but a few days after his transfer, he began to take a turn for the worse again. The doctors tried many of the same treatments the doctors in the previous hospital had tried and failed doing.

My brother expressed his concerns to the doctors, asking them to contact the doctors at the prior hospital. At one point, Jason got so frustrated with their unwillingness to communicate with the previous doctors that he picked up the phone himself. The doctors at both hospitals told him that once a patient was released into the care of another facility, their involvement with that patient ceases. Their hands-off attitude was intensely frustrating. I talked to Jason and heard the desperation, helplessness, and fear in his voice. He knew in his heart Dad was going downhill and there was nothing he could do.

Two days after that phone call, Dad died.

I had been out shopping on that Saturday morning. I came back to my dorm room, only to hear a message on my machine.

It was Mom. She said, "Hi Meg. It's Mom. Call me as soon as you get in. I love you." Her words, spoken through her trembling voice, communicated the dreaded moment. Dad was gone. I knew it in my heart.

I picked up the phone to return her call—only to hear her tears and sorrow on the other end. She told me Dad had died.

"*No!*" I screamed. But that didn't make the pain go away. The anger enraged me. I fell to the floor, throwing the closest object against the wall, leaving a dent. Nothing I could say or do was bringing Dad back. Nothing. He was gone. Despite the rage I felt during all of his drunken nights at home, I still yearned for one more moment with him.

Reality began to hit me hard. I would never have that again. It was the most helpless feeling to watch someone, whom I loved and depended on, dwindle away before my eyes.

My daddy was gone.

My brother had arranged my flight home the next morning. The next twelve hours, I waited. I lay awake all night, surrounded by my friends and several boxes of tissues, yet I had never felt so alone and empty. After hours of crying and searching for comfort from friends, I tried to sleep. I remember lying in bed that night watching VH-1. One song played over and over as the hours crept by. I spent those hours listening to Mariah Carey and Boyz II Men sing "One Sweet Day," (Afanasieff, Morris, Mccary, Morris,

Carey, & Stockman, 1990), a song about meeting a loved one in heaven one day. I look back now and realize God was trying to provide comfort to me—which I had searched for through my friends—through this song. I didn't recognize it at that time, but I believe now it was God's way of letting me know Dad was with Him. I guess that thought was the only thing keeping me sane and stopping me from doing something harmful to myself so I would no longer feel pain.

Isn't it interesting that when we hurt, we often try to resolve pain with more harm?

After many hours of crying had passed, the morning sun finally rose. My wonderful friends, although exhausted themselves, rolled out of bed at five a.m. and took me to the airport. They wanted so badly to find comforting words, but there just weren't any. All I wanted was what I couldn't have—my father's words of comfort.

I boarded the plane, fastened my seat belt, and lay my head against a stiff and unwelcoming head rest. The next thing I remember, the pilot was announcing our arrival into Gainesville. I don't think I had ever slept that well on an airplane before. Why was I able to sleep so soundly on that airplane but could not catch a wink of sleep the night before? Pure exhaustion? Or perhaps being closer to the Prince of Peace? In my twenty years with Dad, I never felt a religious, peaceful side of him until that moment on the plane.

My grandmother claims he was spiritual when he was younger but turned away from God after the early death of his first child,

Amy. Amy became very ill at the tender age of three, and after several days in the hospital, she died. Dad told a vivid story about the day she passed. He said a minister came into the room and told him God had taken her for better reasons and needed her in heaven more than keeping her here.

Dad replied, "Well then, why did He bring her here in the first place?"

At that moment, he turned his back on the minister, and God.

CHAPTER 6

Looking Back to Step Forward

A few days and a few un-eaten casseroles later, Mom, Jason, and I began planning his funeral. We knew Dad would not have wanted a big production full of tears and sorrow, so we chose to have a small graveside service with just family and close friends. Dad had always spoken highly of an old college friend and teammate, Roger. He bragged for years about his athletic career at Johns Hopkins University where he played an attack position on the lacrosse field. He used to get such a glimmer in his eyes when he spoke of his experiences in school and with his lacrosse buddies. We thought it would be special to have Roger speak about Dad's younger years. He spoke of the good times, the practical jokes, and the nights of hanging out with the guys. I had always heard about Dad's wild college days, but it was nice to hear his friend reminisce as well.

I remember standing at the graveside and listening to Roger

share stories of their days on the field together ... but his words didn't seem to make me feel Dad's presence. I told Mom and Jason I wanted to speak as well. My heart pounded while my legs shook as I stood before my family and our close friends. Speaking about my father was one of the most intimidating things I had ever faced but something I had to do.

I looked up and saw Mom crying. I always hated to see people I loved crying, especially Mom. She is a woman who has cared for others her entire life, and I hated to see her sad for any reason. She deserves only happiness.

After Roger finished sharing memories of Dad—the days on the lacrosse field and the good times in college—I stood in front of Dad's grave and looked at my family, ready to share my heart. The pain and loss I was feeling at that moment was tremendous. Dad meant everything to me. Despite his faults and bad choices, he was still my daddy, my mentor. He was such a wonderful man who had carried his hurt for far too long. Unfortunately, that hurt led to bitterness and the bitterness, I believe, ultimately led to his death. It was a distinct message I would deliver. I didn't want this moment to pass without acknowledging Dad's life and his death's purpose, and that purpose was more than just a few good stories.

Like any family, we had our differences. Those differences led to a lot of harsh words, grudges, and wounded hearts. And it was time, *right here, right now* to put the differences and pains aside and step forward in life.

I began by saying Dad was more than a father. He was a

teacher, a mentor, a comedian, a husband, and a friend. He had such a demeanor about him … he knew when someone needed to laugh … and when someone needed to cry. He taught me how to be a good person, to respect myself and others. He taught me to stand up for what I believe in and when to throw the cards in; learn when to pick your battles. One of his favorite songs, Kenny Rogers' "The Gambler" depicts my dad's outlook on life. I had learned so many things from him and didn't realize or at least appreciate it until after he died.

The purpose for his life became clearest through his death.

I vividly remember hearing the ongoing arguments between my dad and some of his relatives during my childhood. My focus was not, "Why are they fighting," but rather, "When are they going to stop?" I was emotionally drained and tired of walking on eggshells in my own home. At times it seemed the children of the family were more mature than the adults. I had always struggled to understand how people who claimed to love each other so much could be so hurtful to one another and hold grudges over the most insignificant things.

In her book *Hurt People Hurt People,* Dr. Sandra Wilson writes, "Rather than acknowledging the existence of our invisible inner injuries and treating them, we often attempt to distance ourselves from them by deflecting our pain onto those around us" (Wilson, 2001, 31). And many times the people doing the hurt are family members; sometimes it's intentional but more often it's not. Through the course of his life, my father did just that: distanced himself in order to deflect pain or opposition. His method of operation was the "silent treatment." And he wasn't the only one in our family to utilize this dysfunctional technique. I have fallen into the same trap.

But as I stood over his grave, I reflected on how that pattern had to stop. Now. My father always instilled the importance of speaking my mind and not to fear the response.

So on the day of Dad's funeral, as I stood beside his urn, I decided to take this opportunity to do exactly that: speak my mind. If ever they would receive the message that life is too short to continue patterns of hurt, it was now. I have heard the cliché that every day is precious but never appreciated the statement until this moment. Dad's passing was an awakening to that very lesson—don't let opportunities pass by without sharing *what's in your heart and what you've learned* from your mistakes.

I closed my eyes and the words, along with the tears, came pouring out. While my heart searched for the courage to express my final thoughts, my brain gave me the words to share my memories and *the message*. I had only hoped that what I was saying would be heard, digested, and put into action.

There are so many times when we take the people in our lives for granted. Though I didn't understand the complexity then, I now know God creates us and specifically chooses the people in our lives because He knows how they will be an integral part of who we are. And yet, instead of being grateful for all our experiences, both good and bad, we tend to dwell on the negative and hurt the people who are most important to us.

I felt as if Dad had finally accomplished something he'd

struggled with the last years of his life: forgiveness and making peace. I genuinely felt these words came from my mouth but had been sent to my heart from my father. *I was simply the vessel, not the messenger.* It took him facing death to realize the time he had wasted holding grudges and playing mind games. When I finished speaking, I looked up.

There wasn't a dry eye.

We all cried, hugged, and began to move on with our lives. However, as I have learned in my life, unforgiveness will find its nasty way of working itself back into the picture. I wish I could conclude this chapter of the book with a feel-good, romance-novel-type ending. But in reality, unforgiven pain and unfinished hurt is just that. Unforgiven and unfinished. And there's still a lot of it in my family, maybe yours too.

The time came when we had to face the harshest reality of all. Life must go on. Mom, Jason, and I picked up our heads, took deep breaths, and began living again. It was amazing how the outside world disappears when you experience something of this magnitude. The TV had not been watched and the newspaper not read, and we still managed to know what was happening in the world. People were living happy, sad, exciting, and dull lives. The chapter in my life was still the same focus—school—although I now took it a little more seriously. After spending the first two years of college skating-on-ice academically, I finished my junior year by making the Dean's List. I attribute this accomplishment to Dad. After experiencing this loss, my priorities became well-defined. Parties became less interesting. Friendships took on a new significance. I enjoyed the times with my friends, for I realized that one day, our togetherness would come to an end as well. And through this experience, my desire to help others through difficult times grew.

I guess subconsciously I wanted to do it for Dad because he had done so much for me. That summer, Mom and I spent time together while Jason pursued his duties with the army. We tried to relax and enjoy each other's company. It was difficult living in a house that held memories of Dad; it was also comforting feeling him around us. I enjoyed it, but was ready to move forward in life and "get out into the real world."

CHAPTER 7

Life in the Surreal World

When many young men and women take their first steps into "the real world," it is a time of joy, excitement, anxiety, and hope. I, just as many, had a desire to "save the world" ... or at least make it better. Little did I acknowledge that the world isn't always as fixable as we'd like.

With graduation from college just around the corner, life in the real world was creeping in. I needed a job. I applied for a position as a mental health assistant in a hospital in Greensboro. The particular clientele associated with this position were children ages four to twelve years old. Not really knowing what the duties were, I applied anyway. I knew I had a love for children and a want to help others. I submitted my resume, and within one week, I was called for an interview. I remember walking through the hospital doors, hoping my interview would be successful and I would be employed immediately. It's a scary feeling being fresh out of college, not really understanding what the world is all about but trying to fit in anyway.

I talked with the director, Mr. "Brown", about what the position entailed. He told me the children at the hospital suffered from many psychological, environmental, and behavioral problems. As the interview went on, my intrigue grew. I sensed this was where I wanted to be. It was clear this was the job for me. Despite my feelings, doubt still entered my mind. I was young and insecure. *Did they like me? Was I qualified? What could I have said differently? When will they call?*

Just a few days after my interview, Mr. Brown called back. "Hi, Meg. How are you?"

I responded cordially, "Hi, I'm great. How are you?" *Just tell me!* I thought.

He proceeded to say they had been very impressed with me. *Well?* I thought.

"And," he continued, "We would like to offer the position to you with the second-shift staff on the children's unit."

"Great! Thank you!" I was ecstatic and could hardly believe this opportunity. I loved children and I loved helping. What a perfect fit!

As I concluded my days at Elon by walking across the stage under the oak trees to accept my diploma, I remember it feeling bittersweet. I was proud of my accomplishments but heartbroken Dad wasn't there to put his arms around me, wink at me and say, "Way to go, Meg. I'm proud of you and I love you."

On that day I wore a necklace with a locket containing a picture of Dad. After I crossed the stage to return to my seat, I remember looking up to the sky, grasping the locket in my right hand as a tear dropped down my cheek to say, "Thanks, Dad. I love you too."

I was excited about the future that lay ahead. I was excited to change the world, one child at a time.

Only a week after graduating, I walked into the children's unit at 3:30 p.m., the start of my shift. I was introduced to several of the other employees. Gary, one of the other mental-health assistants on the children's unit, introduced me to my co-workers. There was an unusual man—Jack—standing behind the nurses' station. After introducing himself, he puzzled me with his first question. "Meg, do you know what the mascot is for the children's unit?"

I thought. *What kind of person is this, and why is he asking me this?* I noticed the others smiling at his remark. *Was I becoming the butt of the joke on my first day of duty?* I responded, with slight sarcasm, "Well, I heard it's you." Laughter instantly erupted from the other staff members, the peanut gallery.

I was in.

As I continued working over the next year, I primarily worked with Jack and Gary. Our working relationship was much like the first time we met: serious when necessary, with doses of humor and sarcasm mixed into moments of lesser intensity.

I discovered this type of humor was common in this profession. It took the edge off the seriousness of the job. Mental health is a tricky and demanding field. It takes a great deal of insight, patience, care and a certain degree of mistrust toward patients. Sometimes behavior, particularly in children, appears to be something completely opposite of the emotion a person is experiencing. This work challenged me every day. It was like attempting to put a puzzle together without looking at the top of the box. Trying to figure it out and not knowing how many pieces there really were and whether these pieces really interlocked the way they appeared to or were masking something deeper.

I spent my afternoons and evenings talking with kids who were dealing with mental health issues. I was amazed and astounded at the number of children who are diagnosed and medicated for some major psychological issues—depression, attention deficit hyperactivity disorder (ADHD), and obsessive compulsive disorder (OCD), to name a few. After growing up in a relatively easy environment, raised by two parents who encouraged us to openly and honestly talk about anything and everything, it was difficult for me to understand the issues these children were coping with. *What could a child who has only seen the world for five or six years possibly have to be depressed about? Why don't children tell adults when they are sad, instead of beating their baby brother, sister or even their own beloved pet?*

I learned a lot about human beings, especially the mind of a child. Many times, a child displays actions that send the message he or she is angry, when in actuality the child is sad and does not know how to effectively express that emotion. "She's been beating up on her little sister." "She tried to flush the cat down the toilet." "He won't sit still." "He likes to play with fire." "He sees the Devil when he sees red." The list went on and on. Some of these kids did have some serious psychological issues and, in some cases, medications were effective. But the majority, from my perspective, just needed some structure, security, three good meals every day, and someone to talk to. More importantly, they thirsted for someone to genuinely care about them. Many were the product of a severely dysfunctional home.

Oftentimes punishment is used against the aggressive behavior, but the underlying reason, the sadness, is overlooked and unaddressed. As tender-hearted as I am, I believe when a child's heart stays broken, it is unacceptable. This was, by far, the most difficult part of the job—knowing some of these kids would probably live most of their childhood and maybe most of their lives in a home where their emotional needs were not a priority. I wanted to take many of these kids home with me and show them they are worthy of being loved and respected.

Two children in particular found a place in my heart.

At the age of six, this little boy, "Sam", had already begun to hate women. His mother had physically, sexually, and verbally abused him. What reason had she *given* him to trust a woman? His parents had recently divorced, and he now lived with his dad. His father tried to help his son, but the abuse had been so bad, Dad turned to us for help. After his father finished with the admission process for him, Sam was brought to the children's unit.

Jack, Gary, and I had been briefed by the intake counselors on Sam's background, and Jack instructed me to focus my attention on this little boy. "As far as you're concerned, he's your only patient," he directed.

We had to show this little guy that women are not enemies,

even though his mother had already given him that impression. I was extremely nervous but at the same time anxious to show him the healthy, nurturing side of women.

He came into the unit and immediately put up a guard when he saw me. I knew I had a difficult task ahead, but the effort would be well worth it when I succeeded. And I truly believed I would be successful. It was what I was there to do—help.

He was in the hospital for the next three weeks. It took a lot for him to open up to me, but over time, he finally came around. After hours of trying to convince him women are not the enemy, he finally made a cry for help. I was working one weekend with another female nurse who only worked weekend shifts. She had not seen the struggle we had been through over the weeks of his hospitalization. He was lying in his bed asleep. I was standing at the nurses' station.

All of a sudden I heard, "Megan!" I went running in the direction of his frightened voice. Sam continued screaming my name until I arrived at his bedside. He was terrified. He'd had a horrible nightmare. When he woke from it and wanted comforting, he called for me. A woman. I could not believe it. I had made a breakthrough in his little life. He finally trusted women, or at least one. I laid him back in his bed, read him a book, and watched him doze into a restful sleep again. It was the most rewarding night I had experienced working in the hospital. He had a need, and I met it.

I walked back down the hallway toward the nurses' station. I was elated. After I sat down to make a note in his chart, the charge nurse on duty that weekend, "Leona", told me I was getting "too attached" to the patients and my behavior was unprofessional. *What?* I thought. If she only knew what I had gone through to reach the point I had just experienced.

It was times like these that gave me the inspiration to come back to work each day. I had talked to my mom earlier. Without revealing any confidential information, we discussed, in general, some of the issues these kids faced. She was astounded and amazed at what some of these children were already dealing with so early in their lives. She asked, "How do you do this every day?"

I said, "Mom, it's amazing. When we stop focusing on ourselves and spend eight hours a day on someone else's problems, it really puts things in perspective. Our life suddenly doesn't seem so bad."

The second child was an eight-year-old little girl, "Beth." She was beautiful, smart beyond her years, and apparently, depressed. Her mom had been in and out of treatment for drinking and depression. She had been with many different men, never committing to any of them, and couldn't seem to understand why her daughter was sad.

Instability. Uncertainty.

This would make anyone crazy. Adults get bent out of shape when we are delayed by bumper-to-bumper traffic or if our to-do list at work is clouded by an unexpected, urgent task. Imagine how children react when they don't know who will be coming through their front door and what "baggage" he'll bring to the home.

She had begun to act out at home, talked about killing herself, and expressed negative feelings toward herself. She felt as though the problems in her household were stemming from her. She was a brilliant child, with a caring heart and a desire for positive attention.

When she arrived on the unit, I took one look at her and my heart smiled. She was a beautiful little girl but had the eyes of a lost child. I knew she and I would work well together. After a few sessions of one-on-one counseling, she became a different child. She smiled more. She laughed more. She trusted adults. She spent the next week or so eating three meals a day, writing, coloring, smiling, laughing, and playing with her peers. The psychiatrists were dumbfounded. There was nothing "wrong" with her. Group therapy revealed a child who wanted to be loved, stable, and free from carrying adult responsibilities. After meeting her mom and her aunt one night during family visitation, she appeared to me to be the most stable and sound person of them all.

Unfortunately, after a few days in the hospital, she had also been given antidepressants. This was a brutal lesson I learned working in the mental-health field. Medications are often used to make the "situation" better, even if the child doesn't necessarily need them. Shortly after that, she was discharged and sent back into an environment that, I thought, was sure to strip her of this progress. I gave her a hug and told her to remember that she was a special little girl. My heart was sinking. How I wished I could take her home with me and give her the positive attention she so desperately deserved.

Unfortunately, that wasn't reality, and I knew it.

She returned to her mother's home and the cycle continued. A few weeks later, she was re-admitted to the hospital. I truly believed she *wanted* to come back. She wanted simple things in life, to grow up in a safe and nurturing environment, with one mom and one dad. She wanted to play, learn, and grow. But mostly, she just wanted to be loved.

She stepped on to the unit and saw my face. She ran to me and called "Miss Megan!" She smiled and gave me a hug that would have hurt an ox. She had gained a few pounds, which is often a side effect from the medication, but she was still a beautiful child. She gave hugs, laughed, smiled, and helped other kids be kids. This cycle of admission to the hospital and discharge a few days or weeks later continued over several months. We talked about the situation at home. It infuriated me to think of the environment she dealt with in her own home. Through additional one-on-one conversations, she described her life at home. Her mother was so focused on herself, she didn't offer anything positive for her daughter. She only responded when she had done something wrong. After another dose of positive attention from the hospital staff, and, much to my dismay, an increase in medication, she was back on her way. This time I wished her well and told her to talk to her mother about how she felt, hoping in the back of my mind I would not see her in the hospital again.

From the lens I viewed her through, she didn't need therapy; she needed a mother who cared. Finally, after what I thought would be the last discharge, I walked into the lobby one afternoon to report for work. There she sat. I sighed in frustration. *This cycle has to stop*, I thought.

"Hi Miss Megan." She came running to me.

I gave her a hug and said, "Hi, sweetie. It's good to see you, but why are you here?"

She paused, dropped her head, and stood silent for a few moments. Then, looking up at me with a tear streaming down her face, she said, "I was raped, Miss Megan."

My heart sank and the tears filled my eyes. I fell to one knee, dropped my purse on the floor, and wrapped my arms around her.

To this day, more than fifteen years later, I still cry when I think about that moment.

I immediately got one of the intake counselors to see her. They checked her in and her mother left. When she stepped onto the children's' unit and saw the male nurse, whom she had known before, she immediately clung to me. She was terrified of men, and through this simple action, it was apparent to me at that moment that her rape really did occur, and this hospitalization was not a ploy for attention, but a plea for help. However, to be certain, one of the nurses escorted her to the local medical hospital to confirm the allegation through a rape test, which was positive.

Later that evening, we sat together and talked. She shared that she had been at one of her friend's house and the older brother was there. He was sixteen. She said her friend went out of the room and the older brother started to talk to her, convincing her to go into the basement and look at some kind of game. Little did she know the game involved stealing her innocence. He pinned her down and took her most precious gift, *trust*.

For the next few weeks, I worked with her, encouraging her to talk to and trust the male employees. I remember her breakthrough day like it was yesterday. One of the older boys on the unit had been saying some hurtful things to rile her. She communicated her anger and her hurt to me but was terrified to approach him. I finally convinced her to stand up for herself, that I would be *right by her side* to support her.

The hours crept on that evening, and she finally built up her nerve. "I want to talk to him, Miss Megan."

"Okay, I'll go get him. It'll be okay, sweetie," I assured her.

I brought him to a common-area room, sat two chairs across from each other, and sat by her side. For the next thirty minutes she told him, specifically, what he had said, why it was hurtful, and why she had been afraid of him given her recent horrible event. She said she expected an apology. I had *never* seen anything like this, not even from adults. She was amazing. She was brave. She was strong. She stood up for herself. She was honest.

And, she got her apology.

The next day, she was discharged from the hospital. Though I've never seen her again, I'm sure she's handling life just fine. She's too strong not to.

CHAPTER 8

Judgment Day

Several months following Christopher's death on March 4, I resigned from the hospital. The stress of working there had become too much, the memories of that night too vivid. I welcomed the opportunity to step away. I accepted a job at a local gym working in the nursery. The investigation regarding the patient's death was still ongoing. Each person involved that night had been advised to seek our own legal representation. I never thought any criminal charges would happen because I truly believed, and still believe, we did everything in our power to help the patient, not hurt him. But, I took their advice and hired an attorney anyway. Through a referral from a friend, I contacted David for a consultation. During our initial conversation over several hours, I recounted the events of March 4. David listened, took extensive notes and agreed to represent me.

Over the course of several months during the investigation, I learned a lot about the legal process, human motivation and the power of choice. I believe that choice is a gift that that every person possesses. As with any gift, we may cherish it or abuse it. Sometimes what appears to be the right decision is actually just the easy way out. On March 4, I chose to go to work. I chose to respond to the call of the code one. I chose to use a towel, based on my training, knowledge, and experience. After the death, I was repeatedly asked, "If you could change anything you did that night, would you?" The only honest response I could offer was, "I wouldn't have gone to work."

Several more people were tested on their use of this power. The detectives could choose to spin the evidence to assign fault, or they could recall the event as it was told to them. The district attorney also had a choice—to pursue an indictment toward the people involved with the restraint or to not prosecute. The media played a crucial role during this time. They hounded the DA. The story was making national headlines, and reporters from *60 Minutes* were knocking on the door. The pressure from the media was intense on me and the DA's office.

The DA's career was going strong, after serving his first term as district attorney. Re-elections were upon him, and his campaign had stirred a stronger interest in many in the community. This case was the driving force behind his latest public appearance. The press wanted the exclusive story. The people wanted an answer about the cause of this death. So did I. I just never imagined I would be viewed as that cause. A person died and although that was horribly tragic, it didn't imply that someone, that I, was negligent.

After many months of investigation by the police and DA's office, the pressure to pursue a course of legal action was at the top of the DA's list. He had to decide. Was someone at fault for this death? What would be the charge? The DA chose to let the lead detective present the case to a Grand Jury. He *made a choice,* and in my opinion, his decision was largely influenced by the media pressure and his lingering re-election status.

On July 5, after all the fireworks had burnt out, the inferno in my life was just beginning. Our attorneys had told us that the Detective Evans was presenting the case to a Grand Jury, and they would be making a decision about whether or not to indict anyone. I, along with some of my co-workers involved that March night, decided to occupy the time together as we waited for the answer from the Grand Jury. We chose to spend the day at the North Carolina Zoo. We all tried to keep the atmosphere light, but no one could seem to focus on the animals but rather on the animosity we may face. Our cell phones were all within reach, waiting for calls from our attorneys assuring us it was over, that no one was at fault. The beautiful sunny day crept on with no calls. I finally gave my hugs to the others and left because I had to work in the gym's nursery that evening.

As I drove to the gym, I kept my cell phone close at hand. Nothing. I arrived at the gym, changed into the appropriate attire, and headed to the nursery. The television was on, channel 10. Five o'clock hit, and it was time for the evening news. I expected the weather report and the local headlines. I never imagined my name would soon *become* the local headline. Earlier that day,

Detective Evans had stood before twelve people on the Grand Jury, recounting his version of the events of March 4. My attorney later told me he'd spoken for more than two hours about my involvement alone: the towel, the statement. He had convinced the jury of the allegation that my actions on March 4 had been reckless and dangerous.

As I sat in the rocking chair in the nursery, I heard the lead news anchor say, "Authorities have decided that one person is to blame for the death of 'Christopher Stevens' last March". I turned to look at the television and was astounded at what I saw. My name, in bolded letters, scrolled across the bottom of the television screen. The reporter continued talking about me. "She has been charged with involuntary manslaughter for this death".

My heart dropped. I don't remember hearing any children in the nursery laughing or talking. I only heard the sound of my name on the news. I immediately ran to the locker room. A friend and coworker met me there. She too, sat in disbelief and shock. She kindly offered to take my place in the nursery that evening, as it was apparent to her I was in no shape to offer love and attention or take care of the needs of the children in the nursery.

I had new needs of my own.

I gathered my purse and gym bag and rushed home. When I arrived, my boyfriend was on the phone with my attorney. After hurling my gym bag across the kitchen and letting out a scream of disbelief and anger, I picked up the phone. "David, what happened? Why me? I didn't do anything wrong!" I was in hysterics.

In his usual calm and soothing tone, he replied, "I know, Meg. I know. I'm so sorry. I tried to reach you before you saw the news. Meet me at the office in one hour."

I took a breath. "Okay, I'll see you soon."

I called a close friend and gasped as I cried to her. "Why? Why is this happening?" She assured me she was there for me and offered a night's sleep at her apartment after I met with David. I didn't feel comfortable at home—I just knew the reporters would be on their way to catch my reaction on film. They had already covered this event like it was the next world war. I hung up the phone, packed an overnight bag and headed to David's office.

For the next several hours, David explained the legal procedure to me. He tried to reassure me I would get through this. As any good attorney would do, he never sent the message that this would be easy but he did assure me that he would stand by me every step of the way. He knew I needed a sounding board and a friend. David let me cry, let me ask questions, and led me step-by-step through this process. His comfort, support, and sound mind was exactly what I needed. I know now God placed David in my life to be the strength I needed.

And David always had a box of tissues for me.

Something beyond my control had occurred, and now I had a choice as to how to respond. I had watched my father respond negatively for years. When faced with opposition, he became angry, hurt, and bitter. He never tried to hurt anyone; he just didn't want to be hurt anymore. My father's words replayed over and over in my mind. "Stand up for what you believe in Meg". At that moment, I knew I only had one option.

To stand up for what I believe in.

After my meeting with David, I went to my friend's apartment. I don't think I slept a wink that night. The next morning, David met me at his office. During our previous meeting, he explained that I had to voluntarily turn myself in to the local jail for fingerprinting and a mug shot. So, there I sat on a hard wooden bench in my khaki skirt suit, aligned next to many other "accused" people who didn't exactly present themselves in a respectable way. I remember looking over in David's direction as he stood next to the ADA, who would later try this case. He looked at me sitting next to the others on the bench, turned to David and said, "She doesn't exactly fit in, does she?"

The sheriff stepped into the waiting room and called my name. I grabbed my purse and headed back into the fingerprinting area. After I washed the ink off the tips of my fingers, he positioned me in front of the camera.

He looked down at the paperwork and said, "Are you the girl from the hospital?"

"Yes." I replied.

The look on his face spoke a thousand words; he didn't believe in the charge either.

I asked, "Can I smile for this picture?"

He paused. "In all the years I've been doing this job, no one has ever asked me that."

I explained, "Maybe that way, the reporters won't flash my

picture on the news." It was a desperate attempt to avoid more exposure of me as this horrible person they had been so eager to portray.

Before the arraignment, David had negotiated my release with the ADA. Following the finger printing and mug shot, I headed home. I had to begin facing this situation. My phone rang off the hook with reporters calling to "get my side of the story." My attorney advised me to decline all interviews until the trial was over for fear that *anything* I said could be used out of context. Though very scared, I was anxious for the trial. I wanted to tell my side of the story.

But I would have to wait for the right time to tell it.

As he prepared for my trial, David approached me and shared his concerns about the amount of investigation that this case would require. He explained that as a sole-practitioner, he felt that it was too much for him to handle alone. So he asked for my permission to add his colleague to my defense team. I agreed and Locke joined our efforts to get to the bottom of what happened.

They are like night and day, both in appearance and personality. David presents himself very calm, cool, collected and focused. I learned not to interpret this demeanor as anything but reserved and intensely thorough in his work. I remember the first time I stepped in his office. The walls were lined with diplomas, plaques and numerous awards from his days working as a federal prosecutor. David's quiet persona is only the calm before the storm in the courtroom. When he needed to be aggressive in his professional role, nothing would stop him from getting to the bottom of an issue.

Locke is the modern-day Matlock. In his white and light blue, pin-striped suit, he is nothing less than an anxious tiger waiting to be released from his cage into the courtroom. More extroverted than David, Locke does not shy away from any opportunity to tell you what he thinks. He too, had a lengthy track record for success in the legal field. People know who he is, and what he is capable of in court.

Though very different, I would spend the next several months witnessing just how strong, qualified and professional they both are. David and Locke are without question, a legal powerhouse together.

And thank God, He put both of them in my path.

There were so many questions that needed answers. Did the patient's medical history indicate any other underlying medical conditions that may have caused his death? Did the use of medications play a role in the death? Were my actions, according the law, reckless or negligent in any way? What was the true cause of death?

David and Locke questioned experts in the field of psychotropic medications. They interviewed other medical examiners regarding the autopsy report, asking them specifically to explore what evidence the body revealed about why he died. They met with experts regarding the use of restraints. They spent months, tirelessly, working on my behalf. To the best of their efforts, they tried to reassure me that this case was full of unanswered questions; questions that they would seek answers to. From the moment they met me and I them, we were a team.

Unfortunately, while I felt security from my attorneys, my relationship with Jim began to decline. As the stress of this trial increased, our relationship was beginning to fall apart at the seams. This was largely due to my focus. The lens I looked through was heavily focused on my circumstances, and I was the center of this pity party. I distanced myself from many friends, became depressed, mistrusting, unfulfilled, angry, and most of all resentful.

Why me? I questioned.

If there really is a God, how could He let this happen to me?

CHAPTER 9

The Trial

On Monday, April 19, 1999, jury selection began. One by one potential jurors were seated in the jury box and questioned by the ADA and my attorneys. I began to appreciate the process of jury selection as a delicate, purposeful process. After several hours, twelve jurors were selected. I would later learn just how significant these twelve people would be, specifically one in particular.

The ADA spoke first. He approached the jury and gave his opening statement. He gave his best account of what had happened. But as I sat and listened, I couldn't help but think his heart was not truly into his theory. His mannerisms and words were telling two different stories. I had this feeling in my gut that in some way, he didn't really think I was responsible for this death. But, just as we were accountable to do our job on March 4, he also had a job to do. He had to try this case.

He reminded the jury that the charge of involuntary manslaughter does not involve intent. I think he was trying to make those twelve people believe that although we had good intentions, we —or rather I—had taken the life of a young man and was to blame. It angered me to hear this message because in reality, our actions were to *prevent* this type of outcome. After all, it was our reason for being at work that night and all the numerous nights before March 4.

We were there to help.

The prosecuting attorney took his seat, and my attorneys took charge. They took turns defending my name, my actions, and my role. Through words, David painted a picture of me—who I was as a person. He focused on my willingness to help those in need and my love for helping kids.

At the conclusion of the day, we left the courtroom and went home. Still very much focused on the situation, I felt so isolated, so alone, even though my family was nearby. With each passing moment, I felt myself slipping into a deeper pit, one I didn't know how to escape. I was bound by my limited perspective.

That changed on April 20, 1999. At the conclusion of day two of my trial, I anticipated going home, turning on the five o'clock news only to hear my name butchered by reporters.

Then something happened to change the focus.

Columbine. The shootings. The deaths. The devastation portrayed on the terrified faces of numerous teens about what had just happened. The questions. Why? How could anyone do this? How could anyone be so hateful and filled with so much rage? How could a teenager plan and act with such intent to destroy the lives of so many innocent people? How could the parents survive the losses? Why would a young person bring a gun to school? Why would they take the lives of so many, of their peers, and hurt the lives of so many more who loved them?

Perspective. Focus. Mine instantly changed, all in the click of a television remote. Suddenly my problem, my trial, seemed to take a seat in the back row of my brain. It was still important and scary, believe me, but following that newscast, my pity party had fewer balloons. Part of me really wanted to jump on a plane to Colorado and hold the hands of so many who were hurting. My heart felt for all of the moms and dads who would never see their kids alive again. My soul ached with tremendous sadness for the mothers and fathers of the kids who had made this unimaginable choice to take the innocent lives of so many others. How could those parents even begin to understand why their children had become so full of hate, rage, and capable of this kind of destruction?

As the next few days of the trial pushed ahead, I could not help but remember those images on the news. How were they coping? How would the people who lost their daughter, son, friend, or classmate cope?

I looked back in the rows of pews in the courtroom where my family sat. Not just Mom and Jason. My aunts and uncles from all over the country had come to support me. Between this new perspective, family support, and my belief in my innocence, part of me knew I would not only be able cope with this struggle, but I would learn from it too. Even in our darkest, Columbine-moments of life, there is still hope. And finding that hope can change a person's perspective; it can help to ease the pain, even for a moment. The horror of the Columbine shootings altered a lot of people's focus in life. Maybe temporarily, maybe forever. Mine changed instantly. The lens I viewed my situation through became a little less intimidating; it gave me a dose of courage to cope with the adversity I faced at that time.

Over the course of the next six days, the facts of the case unfolded. And this question—what had really caused his death—was closely examined. My attorneys spent months preparing for trial, interviewing experts and trying to gain enough information to show the jury that the medical examiner's opinion regarding the cause of death was wrong. Experts in the fields of psychotropic medications, restraints, and seizures gave their professional opinions about how the patient's history of seizures as child, combined with the numerous medications he was prescribed, could have interacted to cause this sudden death. They picked apart the less-than-thorough medical examiner's report which, in their opinion, lacked any evidence of asphyxiation. They interviewed the EMTs who responded to the call and questioned them about what they'd seen, what they did, and how they tried to revive him. They asked some of my coworkers about what they saw on the night of March 4. They probed them about their actions and asked them to share how this restraint was different from hundreds of others they were involved with.

One of my coworkers, "Debbie", the RN on the adolescent unit, also testified about that night. She told the jury about her telephone conversation with the psychiatrist who was treating Christopher in the hospital. She told him how out of control he was.

She tried to portray the picture of what we were experiencing—the intensity—and the need for help from the doctor.

"Can you give me an order for a chemical restraint?" she asked him.

He responded. "No. He needs to learn how to calm himself down without medicine."

She told the jury she felt helpless and angry with the psychiatrist, "Dr. Carter." So we were left to deal with this out-of-control and dangerous patient.

My attorneys questioned me. I sat in the witness chair for almost two hours. My attorneys interrogated me about every detail of that night. I recalled it, fact by fact. It was painful to recount. It stirred so much emotion in me, years of emotions dating back to the day my father died. But as painful as it was, the day had finally come for me to share my story. And as much as the jury was eager to know what happened, I was desperate to understand it too.

In my effort to do so, David reminded the jury that I had not tried to withhold anything and, that over the course of months leading up to the trial I had been questioned repeatedly by the detectives. My story never changed.

When asked if I heard Christopher say anything, my response was, "Yes, I heard him say, 'I can't breathe.'" David told the jurors I could have just lied and no one would have known better. But I didn't. After my attorneys asked their final question, it was the prosecution's turn.

I will never forget it.

He approached the witness stand. I think he was more nervous than I was. In his shaking hands, he handed me a towel, one similar to the towel used that night. He asked me to fold it in the same way I did that night. I did. And then I handed it back to him. His hands still shook. He asked me a few more questions. That was it. His cross-examination was over. I don't know the exact time, but it felt like fewer than ten minutes. I could not believe it. I expected to be drilled with questions for hours.

A few days passed and closing arguments were presented to the jury. Locke concentrated on the charge at hand and the unbelievable *lack* of evidence that led to the *alleged* cause of death. The ME's report and his testimony which asserted that he based his theory of the cause of death—asphyxiation due to external airway blockage—on the detective's statement that a towel was involved with the restraint, not on *any* anatomical findings on the body. No towel fibers in his lungs and no external evidence of the presence of a towel on his lips or face. *Nothing* on his body showed that a towel was even involved. He assumed a cause of death because he couldn't find—or possibly didn't explore—other causes.

Locke reminded the jury, several times, that the ME's testimony reinforced the notion that he didn't know, from looking at the body, that a towel was involved in the restraint. This piece of the puzzle had come from the police officers; *they told him* a towel was involved in the restraint. To illustrate the point further, Locke wrapped a towel around his head and continued talking to the jury for several minutes. He asserted that his breathing was not hindered at all. After the dramatic presentation, he removed the towel and prompted this question. "So how could the lack of anatomical evidence of the towel's existence be proven as the *source* of the alleged cause of death?" Locke continued his closing remarks and spoke about the fact that no one in the history of North Carolina law who worked in the medical field had been criminally charged for this type of death. And now, during an election year, I was the first.

He portrayed the patient as he was, violent and out of control. He presented his medical history that entailed seizures as a young child. He spoke of the numerous group homes he had been placed in for his behavior over the sixteen years of his life. He wasn't a typical teenager with typical problems. He was different, and he was dangerous. And we were responsible for the safety of *every* person in that hospital.

As I stated previously, the charge of involuntary manslaughter, which carries a maximum sentence of four years in prison, implied that my actions were an improper use of "reasonable care" and were "negligent." The irony of the whole situation was that if we, if I, had done nothing to intervene, to try and stop him from hurting himself, *that* would have been negligent. So we were damned if we intervened and damned if we didn't.

We *had* to act.

Our experts gave a scientific explanation of the true cause of his death. Prior to being admitted, Christopher had been prescribed several psychiatric medications for his various issues. The most plausible explanation for his death, given the evidence, was that interactions of the medicines—the toxicology combined with his history of seizures, and the level of agitation that he experienced—caused a massive seizure which led to his death. *Not one single person or one single factor had caused his death.*

Just hearing those words and truly getting to the truth was an overwhelmingly and amazingly freeing feeling.

There it was. The facts were out. The theories were stated. The jury had to decide. David and Locke had given their best efforts to show that Christopher did not die from reasons one man wrote in a medical examination report. The testimony of each expert poked numerous holes in ME's theory and showed, beyond a shadow of a doubt, that asphyxiation was not the cause of death.

We had to wait and hope our case was as convincing to the jury as it was to me. For the days and months leading up to the trial, I had replayed the events of that night in my head. I repeatedly asked myself, *Did I do this? What could I have done differently? Could I have changed this outcome?* I always came to the same conclusion: *I know I didn't cause this.* I knew what I saw. I knew what I heard. I knew what I had done. My answers to these questions always came back to the same place: I wouldn't have done anything differently, and I couldn't have changed this.

The cause of this death was bigger than all of us.

But would the jury believe it? Though I sat at the defendant's table, I didn't feel like a defendant. Even though our judicial system is set up to view a defendant as innocent until proven guilty, the reality of our culture doesn't always see defendants through that innocence lens. We tend to pass judgment on the person accused, labeling them as a "wrongdoer" or "bad" person. And that description didn't fit what I felt inside. I knew in my heart I had done nothing wrong and that I was a good person who was just trying to help.

The judge read the instructions to the jurors. Although the jurors already knew the burden of proof was on the prosecution, the judge repeatedly emphasized that if they had *any reasonable doubt*, they had to render a "not guilty" verdict. He dismissed the jurors and then dismissed us to a conference room.

There I sat. There I thought and wondered. What price would I pay for standing up for what I believed in?

I would have to wait and see.

CHAPTER 10

Fifty-Three Minutes

I was certain I had done nothing wrong on March 4. The question now became, was the *jury* certain? The clocked ticked as loudly as my heart pounded. During the course of my life, I felt pretty confident in my intentions. I believed I was a good person. I knew I only had a desire to help. I knew a stronger cause, well beyond my control, was the reason for this loss. None of that offered any reassurance that the jury would do what was right. They were human and therefore imperfect. They had not been there that night. My thoughts raced. *Did our defense make it well known that I did not cause this death? Would the jury even consider other possibilities?*

This lack of control created an abundance of fear.

My heart raced. My stomach churned. Never in my life had such a fear of uncertainty consumed me. My fate waited. I worried about the judgment of the jury. I cried. I prayed to a God I didn't know. I felt so isolated, even though I sat amongst many who loved, supported and believed in me. My family and friends searched for words of comfort. There were none. They had no idea how it felt to be so criticized. The last year had been a long, agonizing journey, and it was coming to an end. But what would the next chapter in my life hold?

I could have taken a plea bargain, no contest to the charge in exchange for no time served. I could have taken my life. My gut told me no on both accounts. Dad's words rang through my head: "Always stand up for what you believe in." I knew I hadn't done anything wrong, and I had to stand up for myself and stand behind my actions. Would it be enough?

I sat and listened to the sound of my heart beating—throbbing, actually. It seemed to drown out the words of comfort that were being offered by my mother. She knew she had raised a good daughter and person, but would that be enough to sustain me? To sustain her? My brother was quiet … a sign he was holding in his fear to be strong for me and my mother.

My boyfriend sat with his hands folded in his lap and his head held low. What had this experience done to my relationship with him? He was a cop. He was trained to mistrust "defendants." Why didn't he say anything to comfort me? What could he have possibly said?

The clocked kept ticking … seeming louder and louder with each stroke. The reporters outside the conference door were feasting on my misery. *How could they be so inhumane? Didn't they realize their story stemmed from agony?* The agony felt by a mother and father who had taken this child into their home to give him a new life. The agony of a young woman just trying to help. Agony of the jury being forced to make a decision about a stranger's future.

Did they even care about people? Or were they just trying to make the headlines? They were so emotionally removed from the story they couldn't even pronounce my last name correctly. I could not understand that mentality. My job *required* me to pay attention to every last detail of the children, their names, faces, expressions, and words. The kids were always my top priority.

My thoughts were interrupted when the conference room door flew open. David stepped into the room, looked me in the eyes with a neutral expression on his face. Only these words came from his mouth, "Let's rock and roll." Fifty-three minutes from the time I'd walked into the conference room, the jury had reached a verdict. My thoughts continued to race through my mind. *Was it too soon? Did this mean bad news? Could it have been good news? Was I prepared to hear it?* My thoughts continued to flood my mind.

We settled back into our seats in the courtroom. The bailiff escorted the jurors into the jury box. I studied their faces … nothing. No indication. *What did they decide? Why won't they look at me? Could this be happening? Am I in a bad dream?*

The bailiff spoke. "All rise." I could barely feel my legs, never mind stand on them. My heart pounded faster. My palms were clammy. *This has to be a nightmare. I will wake up soon.*

The judge entered. He didn't look at me. He didn't look at any of the attorneys. *What did this mean? It couldn't be good.* Negative thoughts began to take over the confidence of knowing I had done nothing wrong. It's amazing how influential our thoughts and emotions can be. After the judge sat down, we followed. I welcomed the chance to sit, to take a breath.

The judge spoke. "Will the defendant please stand?"

I tried once again to find the strength in my legs. David offered a hand to help me up. I was going to be sick.

The judge looked across the courtroom and asked the jurors if they had reached a unanimous decision.

"Yes, we have, Your Honor," the foreperson said. Ironically, the foreman was a woman who worked in the mental health field. She had been involved in restraints. She knew the intensity of the situation. And now she was the leader on a jury who would decide if my actions were criminal.

She turned to look at me and turned back to the judge. "On the charge of involuntary manslaughter, we find the defendant"— an eternity passed in a matter of a few breaths—"not guilty."

I dropped to my chair. My body released with a rush of tears. I lost all control. The next thing I remember was looking back at my family, sitting on the hard benches behind me. They too were weeping. My mother rushed over to offer a hug. My brother finally exhaled. My family wept. We all gathered back in the conference room behind the courtroom. The attorneys stayed to conclude the proceedings.

"Expungement" became a new word in my vocabulary. This legal term is an order granted by the judge at the request of the attorney to wipe away this entire charge from the records. It's as if the case never existed; it never happened. *It created a clean slate and a new beginning for me.* And, in the state of North Carolina, a person may only be granted one expungement per lifetime. Locke brought the paperwork to me to sign. My hands shook while tears fell down my cheek as I wrote my name on the blank line.

We stayed in the conference room, hoping the vultures outside would move on to the next breaking news event. David and Locke entered the room with us. I could finally shed tears of *joy*. David handed me some more tissues. "Megan Elizabeth," David said, "let's go." I hugged him and melted into his arms. I felt the first sensation of peace in more than a year.

As we left the courthouse, heading back to David's office, Jason walked on my left side, and Jim walked on the right. They both held my arms to support me. I was exhausted. The reporters swarmed around me like angry bees. Microphones were shoved in front of my mouth. Questions were flying through the air. I ignored most of them. However, there was one question I just couldn't resist answering.

"Megan, do you have anything to say to the jury?" One reporter asked. The other questions became silenced.

I stopped walking, paused to gather my thoughts and said, "Thank you. You were right." I didn't cause this death and they got it right.

Days following the trial, my attorneys were allowed to speak with the jurors. Their conversation with one juror in particular was chilling. She told them that at the onset of deliberation, the jurors took a vote. The vote was eleven to one. One person believed

I was wrong. One person doubted my actions. One person could have changed the course of my future. So what happened? *Heaven* intervened. After the initial vote, one juror stood up and said, "We need to pray about this."

"If cases come before your courts that are too difficult for your to judge—whether bloodshed, lawsuits, or assaults—take them to the place the Lord your God will choose" (Deuteronomy 17:8, NIV).

They prayed. And then they voted again. Twelve people—a unanimous count—voted in favor of my innocence. By the grace of God's outstretched hand, through an act of prayer, I was acquitted. "You saw with your own eyes the great trials, the miraculous signs and wonders, the mighty hand and outstretched arm, with which the Lord your God brought you out." (Deuteronomy 7:19, NIV)

The act of one person changed the course of my future.

CHAPTER 11

Adversity Brings Change

Trials. Opposition. Challenges. While admittedly difficult to endure, adversities serve distinct purposes. The problem lies not in the trial itself but in our reaction to it, our focus. This is so simple, yet we make it so difficult. We want explanations when bad things happen in our lives. Yet when the good times roll, we don't question why. Think about it. Would you be a different person if your mom or dad had never told you "no"? Would NASA have learned and corrected problems with their space shuttles if the *Challenger* had not exploded? Someone didn't just wake up one day and say, "Hey, let's have people ride the same bus and learn in the same classroom, regardless of what they look like." This change occurred after someone took a step toward change, despite the personal affliction she would endure. The idea of racial integration was shot down many times before Martin Luther King Jr. was.

All these changes occurred *after* adversities, trials, and disasters happened. Our lives change when something is put in our path that either shows us we need to stop doing what we are doing, or when something just simply stops us.

My adversity brought a lot of change to my life. I had been living, unmarried, with a man I dearly loved. He was handsome, fun, charming, and hardworking. I just knew we'd be married one day.

That was how I justified living with him. Though neither of us were Christians, we felt on some level that living unmarried together was wrong. As many of us do, we deflected this conviction through jokes about "living in sin." The word *sin* didn't play a role in our lives at that time. But even without a relationship with God—without knowing His Word—it still had a hold on our souls. I just didn't realize it at that time. God wasn't happy we had made an ungodly choice. He knew the only way to really get my attention and get back in His will was to show me His plan for my life.

That plan did not include living a sinful life.

Shortly after the verdict was read, I was on my way home. Back to life. Back to my relationship. When all of this started, I had really hoped things would, at some point, return to "normal." But a few months leading up to the trial, I knew change was inevitable. I just didn't know then, how God would use this trial to better my life.

Though the verdict left me free, I was still bound by depression, uncertainty, and bitterness. I was searching for an escape. I tried to control my feelings through external quick fixes. I tried excessive exercise. I tried to control what I ate, or rather what I didn't eat. I drank, a lot. Do you see the destructive pattern? Do you see the similarity of my efforts to those of my father's efforts to deal with his pain?

All of my attempts to feel whole again left me empty; nothing filled the void. During one of my darkest moments following the trial, I called David. By the sound in my voice, he knew I wasn't okay. At his advice, I sought therapy. He knew this entire experience had been traumatic and left me scarred and deeply scared.

I met with my therapist on a weekly basis. We dug into the depths of how the accusations and the trial had impacted me; it had attacked the very core of who I was. The more we talked, the more I began to realize that this hurt and confusion wasn't going anyway anytime soon.

I just wanted to feel better, and quickly. I wanted to feel whole again. To regain my confidence; to like what I saw in the mirror. I just kept seeing the person the media had portrayed. When the world beats us down, it takes a bigger power to bring us back up. And at that time, I didn't know where to turn for that power, for that strength, to face another day.

It didn't help matters that every time I talked to friends or family, they offered advice to "just let it go and move on." They didn't understand that I *just couldn't let it go*. I had to deal with what had happened and the fact that it had changed me. I had to find a reason to get out of bed each day. I had to figure out the answer to the question, "Now what?" When something that major, that life-altering occurs, you can't just *let it go*. It becomes part of you. It became a moment of change, maybe the most defining moment of my life. My outlook on the world changed. My trust in people changed. I was hurt beyond what I can express in words. Day after day, despite therapy and antidepressants, I grew more and more depressed. I questioned everything, everyone, and every day. I was bitter.

So, so bitter.

I told myself, even before the charges or the trial occurred, that I was finished with work in the mental-health field. I vowed I would never go down this road to help others again. I was too scared to put myself back into that kind of environment, only to find myself becoming a victim of trying to help someone else. I *allowed* fear to paralyze my dreams and passions. I chose to walk another path. And that path, the path to depression and self-pity, only has one direction.

Down.

As I sank deeper into my "pit of poor me," Jim and I grew further and further apart. We both wanted things to get better; we truly loved each other. Love is supposed to conquer all, right? We tried therapy together. I was amazed he actually went to the appointment and was astounded at the level of "stuff", the burdens of life, he also carried.

And of course, my baggage was heavy. All of it surfaced at a time that neither of us seemed to have any strength left to fight for our relationship. Over time, we both changed. We both realized we couldn't go back to the way we were. Too many aspects had been altered. We talked about it and agreed it was time for a break. In July 1999, I moved out. Part of me felt, or maybe just hoped, that we could make it work if we could just give it time and space. But time and space alone don't heal deep wounds.

In addition to moving out, I also moved on to a new career path. I had always had an interest in law. I had taken a few classes in high school, and ironically enough, had played the role of prosecuting attorney for one of my final exams. After seeing how the attorneys, paralegals, and legal staff had helped me through this legal mess, I was intrigued and inspired to try this new career.

Once again, David helped me. He called a colleague of his, a former law school friend, and asked him if he needed any help in his office. I was hired as the receptionist in his small law firm. In addition to working full time, I enrolled in school to become a paralegal. In only ten months, I finished my paralegal certification. Now I was headed for a new beginning. I just didn't know that the new beginning in front of me wasn't about a paycheck but rather a price that was paid for me.

And that price tag had a new, different life attached to it.

CHAPTER 12

My New Beginning

I remember the first night in my new apartment. Following the breakup, I anticipated spending it in tears with a box of tissues and a heavy heart. Much to my surprise, it was the most restful sleep I had had in more than a year. After over a year of dealing with an inner wrestling match with my conscience, I finally rested. Looking back now, I believe that was God's grace and mercy at work. He was trying to show me His plan was better. Unfortunately, I wore such thick blinders; I couldn't even recognize His presence at the time. When I did, many years later, I soon began to experience true inner peace, the peace that only exists when we are on the path to finding God's plan for our life.

A month had gone by since I'd moved out, and my new, independent life was becoming expensive. Despite being hired by a small law firm in Greensboro, I was struggling to make ends meet. I had no one to share the rent with and no one to help carry the financial load of living. My tight budget didn't allow for much wiggle room, so I approached the manager at one of the local gyms. I was hired on a part-time basis two nights a week. The first night I was at the front desk training while greeting gym members. For the first time in my young-adult life, I was honestly not "checking the scene." I was there to do a job, get another paycheck, and reap the benefits of a free gym membership.

Dale, one of the members, introduced himself and went on with his workout. His dark hair, dark eyes, and fit physique caught my eye. He was handsome, no doubt about it. But he left another impression with me, a feeling like none I had ever experienced before. He was full of light and life. It was more than just charm. It was contagious and could fill any room.

Over the next few weeks, Dale made his presence known. His workouts seem to shorten, though he still spent equal time at the gym. He showed interest in me. He spent more and more time standing across the check-in counter from me, just chatting. He inquired about my job in the firm and what brought me to Greensboro. One night, after a long day at the law firm, I was tired, not feeling up to par, and was anxious to go home to bed after my shift concluded at the gym. Dale hadn't come in that night. I had taken note. But, he'd made a point of calling me and asked if I wanted to grab a bite to eat after work. I thanked him, told him I was worn out, not feeling well, and asked for a rain check.

A week later, we were sitting across the table, sipping drinks and sharing our hearts. Over the course of three hours, he told me about his struggles. His marriage. His two sons. His divorce. The hurt, guilt, and pain he had carried for so many years. I sat in awe. To look at him in the gym—his strong physique, his smile, his laughter, his determination—you'd never know he had ever been broken. I was amazed to think that a person could live through that much hurt and still find a way to smile. We started dating in January of 2000 and as the months rolled forward, I began to fall in love with him. We spent so many nights talking about life and I was so intrigued by his spirit that I wanted more of whatever "it" was that gave him such peace and calmness.

I vividly remember so many times he'd tell me story after story about how he and his ex-wife didn't see eye to eye about raising their boys. I would sit back, listening, feeling infuriated and wanting to give my two cents to the situation. I wanted him to get fired up and get mad! Instead, Dale would say, "There's a reason this is happening, and I just have to take a deep breath and pray. God will take care of it." Amazing, if you ask me.

Seven months later, we were engaged. We set a date, April 28, 2001, for the wedding. As the plans moved forward, Dale and I talked about what we wanted out of our marriage—our expectations, hopes, dreams, and children. During my days working on Habitat houses, dealing with my father's death and later the trial, I often turned to Elon's chaplain, Chaplain McBride, for support and guidance. When we announced our engagement, Dale and I asked him if he would preside at our wedding. He happily agreed and told us he wanted us to do some premarital "chatting" with him. As we talked and shared our hearts, God laid a burden on me, one I couldn't shake off or dismiss from my mind. Though I had been found not guilty of the scrutiny I faced in the courtroom, I was undeniably guilty of living a sin-filled life. After months of wrestling with this, God convicted me of my need for a Savior. *Christ* was the hope I had seen in Dale. And I needed that hope too. I needed to accept Christ as my Savior.

After this moment of conviction in late January of 2001, I picked up the phone to call Chaplain McBride. When we spoke I said, "I want to accept Jesus into my heart, and I want to be baptized before the wedding." I explained that it was really important to me that Dale and I were on the same spiritual page before we committed to spend the rest of our lives together. "Can you do it?" I asked him.

"Let me check my calendar," he replied. "Meg, the only date I have available before the wedding is March 4. Is that okay?"

Tears filled my eyes as I thought, *This date, this horrible date that had haunted me for so long was now, by the grace of God, going to have a new memory.*

A new beginning.

"That's perfect" I replied.

"For God so loved the world that he gave his one and only Son, that whoever believes in him shall not perish but have eternal life" (John 3:16, NIV).

CHAPTER 13

Stepping into Step-Motherhood

I wear three rings on my left hand ring finger: one symbolizing my commitment to Dale, and one for each of his boys. I welcomed the chance to not only be a wife but also a step-mother. Standing in front of the church, after exchanging my vows with Dale, I turned my focus toward his two sons. Just as I had promised to love Dale, I also made a promise to his boys.

As I held their hands and looked into their sweet eyes, I said, "I know I'm not your mom, but I promise to love you as a mom, as I would love my own children." And I really meant that. I wanted to be part of their life during the good times and the bad, to celebrate their highs and help them through their lows.

His oldest son, Charlie, then eleven, was the carbon copy of Dale, both in looks and demeanor. He has dark hair, dark eyes, and is vibrantly full of energy. He requires very little sleep and is constantly on the go, so much on the go that at a young age he was diagnosed with Attention Deficit Hyperactivity Disorder (ADHD) and prescribed medication. The doctor who diagnosed and prescribed the medicine? Dr. Carter. A familiar name to me.

It seemed my past was still haunting me.

Dale's younger, eight-year-old son, Parks, was built very different. His blond hair and blue eyes are just some of the surface differences from his older brother. He's a little less energetic, very tender-hearted, and reserved. Dale tells me that from the moment he was born, he was a sleeper ... twelve hours a night do wonders for his attitude.

Though different in appearance and personality, they had one thing in common. Baseball. They spent many hours, days and nights, playing baseball. I was unaware of the commonality among children regarding traveling sports; young kids are spending more and more time traveling to baseball and other sporting events. So much time, it doesn't seem to allow them to experience simple childhoods. I grew up playing outside, exploring in the nearby creek, and telling stories over campfires. Sports existed for me, just not during every waking moment and not at the intensity level of children today.

Though both boys are athletic, Charlie found fascination in building, drawing, solving puzzles, and fishing. He could sit for hours just drawing. During trips to the beach, he would spend his day on the shoreline, net in hand, watching for fish. When given a task that truly tapped into his interest and God-given talents, nothing could divert his attention. From the early days of our marriage and through the years to come, I voiced my concerns to Dale about this ADHD medicine. "He doesn't need it. He's so smart and focused when he's doing something that intrigues him," I reasoned.

To give some perspective to the issue of diagnosing and medication, I shared memories of the children I had seen in the hospital. It appeared to me that ADHD had become the "cookie-cutter" diagnosis for kids who were admitted for behavioral problems. Some of the psychiatrists spent only minutes with the children, made the diagnosis, and ordered the medications.

I remember hearing a comment made by of the psychiatrists while I was working in the hospital one night. "If their parents won't control them, we need to medicate them."

What did he just say? I was stunned and appalled.

As I spent night after night with these kids, I saw a deeper problem, not one curable by medication. Many of these behavioral problems started in the home—the lack of structure and discipline, erratic schedules, unbalanced diets, and the sometimes "out of touch" parents. Most, not all, of these "problems" were fixable through other means: changes in diet, more time playing outside instead of watching the tube, and giving intentional focus on what made the child tick; what they were really passionate about. Just like Charlie, so many un-medicated kids will spend hours doing what they are gifted, talented, and interested in doing and not have a problem sitting still to do it.

After witnessing a small handful of children in the hospital that truly were excessively hyperactive and benefited from medication, I couldn't accept the thought that Charlie fell into this category.

I advocated and voiced my opinion to Dale. "He's just energetic; he doesn't have ADHD. He just needs to spend his energy on the things that fuel his fire and passion."

Dale agreed, and we shared our concerns with Charlie's mom. She disagreed with us and we were repeatedly hit with a roadblock on this subject. I spoke with nurses and doctors I trusted who were experienced in this area of medicine, to ask for guidance. Their advice was that it wasn't safe for Charlie to take this medication periodically. "It's better to leave him on the medicine if you all can't agree. Consistency is crucial."

At that time, the boys' mother had full custody and Dale only had weekend visitations. Given the amount of time spent with her versus the time we cared for them, we knew Charlie would be medicated.

For that reason, with a helpless feeling in our hearts, Dale and I gave in. I felt like we had failed Charlie. And those vows I had said, to care for those boys as if there were my own, lay heavy on my heart and mind.

Over the years of watching the boys grow up and dealing with disagreements from his ex-wife about their well-being, Dale and I dropped to our knees and cried out to God in prayer. Before we married, I had heard stories of other blended families' struggles. As it were, we were now living a life full of those struggles. For years we tried to resolve our differences with the boys' mother through reasonable and rational efforts; efforts that wouldn't require a courtroom. However, we were constantly faced with opposition. So for the boys' best interest, we hired lawyers to fight the legal battle.

Our requests were simple: we wanted more time with the boys and more input about decisions regarding their well-being. The battle would prove itself difficult. Financially, we struggled. Emotionally, we were exhausted. There were days I didn't know how we would make it. It was beginning to tear us apart. Admittedly, there were many days I just wanted to walk away; the stress was so intense. But I couldn't, for a lot of reasons, most importantly because of my commitment to Dale and to the boys.

Following months waiting for our day in court, we finally came to an agreement with their mom. We would split custody. That agreement afforded us more time with the boys and more influence as to any major decisions involving their welfare. *Thank you, Lord.* We were elated! For the first time in more than ten years since Dale's divorce, he finally had the boys on Christmas morning, and many other mornings as well. It truly was a gift from the Lord.

However, time would move forward, and we would face another tough road. I recall one night, in particular. The phone rang; the boys, then in their teen years, called to talk to Dale. As he sat in silence, listening to them on the other end of the line, I watched his facial expression shift from one of joy to one of hurt, despair, and sadness. They called to tell him they didn't want to visit as the schedule had been designed by the court but rather only visit "when they felt like it." They were both involved with traveling baseball and were tired of trucking back and forth between their mom's house and our home, amid their hectic schedules. After all those years of struggling to get more time with them, only to be told they didn't want it, was crushing for Dale and me. In our extremely devastated state of mind, we couldn't help but think their mom had influenced them to make this call. Regardless of the motivation for their decision, we were plagued with a choice. We could fight it and demand they come, or we could let go and trust that one day they would have a change of heart and would come back.

It was a despairing and unbelievably disheartening place for any parent to be.

Once again, I felt myself slipping into a pit of worry, depression, and bitterness. The adversity we dealt with over the course of many years was so painful for Dale and me to carry, so heavy that we *couldn't* carry it. Admittedly, it wore me down.

Thankfully, Dale was again the calm in the midst of what I deemed a storm. He would say, while choking back the tears, "It will work out. God will take care of this."

I so desperately wanted to believe that; to trust God to intervene. We cried; we prayed. Finally, we had *to just let it go*, to trust, and to wait on His timing. It wasn't easy.

It would be years and a lot of difficult moments in the process of waiting before those relationships were restored.

But now, both young adults, they have come back.

"Cast all your anxiety on him because he cares for you" (1 Peter 5:7, NIV).

God is faithful.

CHAPTER 14

Tick Tock, It's God's Clock

Microwaves, fast food, ATMs, instant messaging and on-demand movies—we live in a world of "right here, right now." Somehow, amid all of the "advances in technology" and "overnight deliveries," we've forgotten that the roses still have an aroma. We see them but are too hurried to stop and smell them. One of the most challenging tasks humans face is waiting. I've often joked about not praying for patience because God will truly teach you the meaning of the word.

When our computers don't instantly jump from one screen to the next in .03 milliseconds, we fret. We complain. We whine. Bumper-to-bumper traffic is no treat either. I once heard a minister tell a story about a man who complained about having to sit in his *air-conditioned, leather-seated* car in bumper-to-bumper traffic. He complained about not going fast enough and getting to his destination. Poor thing. How did he even manage to remain calm? But we all do it! We want it yesterday, and when we don't get what we want fast, we find someone to complain to. We scold our children over temper tantrums because they lack patience—maybe we should put ourselves in "time-out" when we can't, or won't, be patient.

I'm not judging others; I'm speaking from experience of being a very impatient person. I am (present tense) among those people who honk the horn at the car who waits, one second after the light turns green, to step on the gas. I can't seem to find the patience to endure the two minutes it takes for popcorn to pop in the *microwave*. If there was a master's degree in waiting, I'd be the first to accept the diploma—not because I'm good at it but because I've had many courses in it.

I've had to *learn* to be patient.

Why do we allow ourselves this constant struggle? Wouldn't it just be easier to sit back, relax, and watch God handle the ticking of the clock? If and when we truly do give timing to God, He provides for us, down to the very last detail. The trouble is, we get frustrated anticipating His answers, and we convince ourselves He's forgotten about our needs, so we take matters into our own hands.

The first lesson He taught me about patience was during the "trying" process of having a child. From the time I was a young girl, I always desired to be a "mommy." After only a few months of marriage, Dale and I decided we were ready to have a child, so I took the necessary "crash course" in reproduction. I managed to become an expert in research. I searched the Internet for information on ovulation, timing, statistics on pregnancy success rates, gender prediction, and on and on and on. "Science" made it clear that our best odds of conceiving were between the twelfth and fourteenth day of my cycle. All the studies on reproduction and gender prediction, number crunching, and "rolling the dice" made me feel like we were headed to Vegas rather than trying to create a *human being*.

After several months of tracking the calendar, having "ideal" relations with my husband, and then anticipating the results of numerous home-pregnancy tests, I continuously found myself in tears over the negative results. Love-making had become a mission ... with a distinct purpose and agenda, exactly what God did *not* intend it to be. I began to feel like I was losing control, as if I ever had it to begin with. Month after month of negative tests, I finally and reluctantly came to terms of letting go of the idea of having a baby. Part of me began to question whether God was somehow punishing me for wrongdoings, for the life I lived before. Which, by the way, God doesn't do. He only offers grace when we have sinned. "My grace is sufficient for you, for my power is made perfect in weakness. Therefore I will boast all the more gladly about my weaknesses, so that Christ's power may rest on me" (2 Corinthians 12:9, NIV).

The Devil, however, was hard at work in my mind. Maybe I *did* do something wrong "that March night," and now I was going pay for it ... oh, how Satan began working on my self-confidence and faith! So I did what we do when we lack patience: I tried to control my inner struggle with impatience through external fixes.

I turned my attention to a different focus: a new job. If I couldn't have a baby, by golly, I was going to have a better job! I had been working as a paralegal in a large law firm for approximately two years and still felt something missing; something was lacking from within. So I applied for a position with the U.S. attorney's office. I mailed my resume and once again waited. More than two weeks passed before I heard any news from the Human Resources department.

I came home one evening from work, expecting nothing out of the ordinary. My husband was already home and my father-in-law was visiting, helping Dale with a home-improvement project in our basement. I went inside, changed my clothes, and greeted them. I went back upstairs to start dinner. I glanced at the kitchen table, where we put the mail each afternoon, and saw that Dale hadn't gotten our mail for the day. I went outside, opened the box, and sifted through the mail. There it was: a letter from the U.S. attorney's office. My heart started to flutter. The negative thoughts consumed me. *It can't be good ... they would have called if it was good.* I went inside and opened the letter.

"Thank you for your inquiry. However ..." It was a closed door. I didn't get the job. Tears filled my eyes. I thought. *This is what I really wanted ... I guess I am still being punished for something.*

My pity party began again.

I sat on the edge of my bed, head hanging low. I thought about why I wasn't getting the things I wanted, or at least what I had convinced myself I wanted. *Is there a reason for this suffering? Why me? God is angry*, I thought. *I didn't get the job ... I'm not going to have a baby and ... wait a minute! It's Wednesday*, I thought. *I usually start my period on Tuesday.*

My body worked like a clock. Always punctual. Maybe my period was just late because of the stress of waiting on this job opportunity. I thought for a moment ... *I have another pregnancy test in the cabinet.*

I walked into the bathroom, pulled the test out of the box, took a deep breath, did the necessary duty, and waited, again. I left the test on the counter and went to check on dinner. I returned to the bathroom a few minutes later. Took another deep breath, closed my eyes, said a silent prayer, and opened my eyes.

Two lines!

Could it really be? I did the next thing that any faithful, "trusting," good little Christian would do (are you sensing the sarcasm?)—I had to make *sure*, 100 percent, without a doubt, in no way that this was a false positive!! I immediately ran to the kitchen to turn off the stove, grabbed my car keys on the way out the door, and yelled to my husband, "I'll be back in a few minutes!" He didn't have a clue what had transpired over the last eight minutes! I drove furiously to the store, ran in, and bought another pregnancy test. The clerk probably thought I was nuts! If this was really it, I wanted confirmation so I would know I hadn't *completely* lost my gourd. Oh wait, it was already too late for that!

When I got back to our house, the result of that second test confirmed it. Two lines! Thank you, God! I thanked Him for the new life growing inside me. And I thanked Him for the letter. It was clear that this was His plan all along, and it was all in His timing. I waited for my father-in-law to leave. I wanted to share this moment with my husband before we shared our joy with our families.

After my father-in-law left, I turned to Dale and said, "Honey, sit down. I have some news. I have some good news, and I have some bad news—which do you want first?"

His big brown eyes looked up at me and he said, "The bad news first."

I handed him the letter. He read the first line and expressed his frustration. "How could you not be qualified?" The anger grew in his voice.

"Wait a minute!" I interrupted. "Here's the good news." I handed him a box wrapped in gender-neutral paper that I had packaged months earlier in anticipation of this moment. He opened it and found the sweetest, tiniest, yellow, footed sleeper pajamas with a zipper front.

Initially, the dots didn't quickly connect in his brain. But after just a few deep breaths, it clicked. He looked up at me and then the sweetest, most romantic words came out of his mouth. "How did this happen?" And really, he honestly meant that in the most excited and loving way possible! He dropped the letter and embraced me with excitement. It was awesome!

But God *still* wasn't finished teaching me about timing.

Over the next nine months, He blessed me and our child with a healthy and uneventful pregnancy. Other than a bad case of stomach flu during my seventh month, my pregnancy was perfect. No morning sickness, no high blood pressure, and I slept "like a baby." (I would soon find out how that saying doesn't really imply a good thing—they don't really sleep very well or very long, for that matter.)

I had reached the eighth month, and my checkup appointments were more frequent but routine. Every two weeks I rotated doctors as the medical practice urged me to do, to become familiar with the other physicians. All of my visits went like clockwork—"Baby's head is down, no dilation yet." I heard this several times.

Three weeks before my due date, I went in for a regularly scheduled visit, expecting nothing other than the same update from the doctor: "Baby's head is down, no dilation yet."

This time it was a different response. The doctor measured my belly, and began the internal exam. With a puzzled look on his face, he said "I'm not sure if what I am feeling is the head or the rear."

Huh? Not sure? I thought. Ten minutes later I was having another ultrasound. Sure enough, my little man was nestled inside me, sitting up tall and proud. He was in a breach, jack-knifed position, with the top of his head resting at the bottom of my sternum.

The doctor began discussing the possibility of turning him. A friend of mine had previously endured this not-so-comfortable process during the latter part of her pregnancy. My mind resorted to what she had shared with me. "It was painful and didn't work." The doctor informed me of the odds of success and the possible risks. If we didn't attempt this, a C-section was the only avenue for delivery. In the previous months, I had gotten a picture in my mind of delivering my baby, feeling the contractions, experiencing the miracle of a natural birth. Surgery had never crossed my mind. I told him I wanted to discuss this with my husband.

That night, we sat and talked. I relayed what the doctor had said. I relayed the story from my friend about her pregnancy. Although I felt within me that this "attempt" was not what God had in mind, I didn't have the peaceful feeling I had experienced during the prior eight months.

The next day, I called my doctor and told him I didn't want to risk the baby's health and that my husband and I had decided on the C-section. I was due on April 18, Good Friday. Due to the holiday and Mom's booked flight in from Florida on the sixteenth, we scheduled the surgery for the seventeenth. Our son, Ayden Bruce, was born on Thursday, April 17, at 1:23 p.m. Due to the surgery, the doctors kept me in the hospital for four days. We brought our healthy, perfect little blessing home on April 20, Easter Sunday. There's no bunny in the world that could ever deliver a better Easter present.

The timing was nothing short of perfection. Why?

"It is not for you to know the times or dates the Father has set by his own authority" (Acts 1:7, NIV).

Because it was God's timing.

CHAPTER 15

GPS

Most cars manufactured today have a built-in GPS (global positioning system), or at least the option to install one. The old days of attempting to read a map or fumble through those large pages of an atlas while driving along the highway are gone. With the modern convenience of simply typing in your preferred destination, the GPS quickly calculates your current location and designs the most accurate roadmap to get you to your final destination. The technology is amazing. With the help of a satellite orbiting in space, the GPS can determine exactly where you are on the planet. And if that isn't cool enough, it also talks to you along the way, giving you ample warning time before each exit you should travel to reach your desired endpoint. Even when you take a wrong turn, the GPS quickly re-calculates where you are and finds the easiest and quickest way to get you back on track.

On a recent business trip, I used a portable GPS, one that plugs into the car, to guide my travels. After several days of meetings and numerous stops in various cities, I was anxious to get home. I entered my address into the system, and it told me how to journey home in the most efficient time and path possible. I was cruising along some country roads, which, according to the GPS, would lead me right onto Interstate 95 south. As I listened to the computerized voice tell me to turn left, I followed the instruction, only to be greeted by a military police officer on an army base! *Clearly*, I thought, *I've made a wrong turn.* At that moment, my faith and trust in the GPS went down the tubes.

In my mind, I questioned why I was on the road.

But with other cars following behind me, and barriers on both sides of the road, turning around wasn't an option. So I continued driving forward, approaching the officer standing at the entrance of the gate. I lowered the driver-side window and said, "I'm sorry, officer, my GPS told me to turn left, and clearly that was an error."

He smiled and replied, "Well, that depends on where you're headed."

I said, "To I-95."

He continued. "Well, then you're headed in the right direction. The road cuts through the base, and on the other side of it is I-95."

After presenting my identification to him, he opened the gate, and I was back on track to getting home.

The GPS was correct. The problem was whether or not I *chose to trust it.*

Just as the GPS guides our travels, God's Provision and

Sovereignty (GPS) in our lives also guides our spiritual journey. My husband and I had been attending a Sunday school class on a regular basis. God has put people in our path along our journey who have nurtured us in our faith walk. When I reached the point where God was leading me to share my journey, to tell this story, one of our Sunday school teachers introduced me to a women's group called Bible Study Fellowship, or BSF. On numerous occasions, she had asked me to go. I resisted. I made one excuse after another excuse not to go. "Monday nights are hard for me." "I feel guilty leaving Dale and Ayden at home after not seeing them all day." "I'm too tired." Finally, after running out of excuses, I gave in. The meetings were held on Monday nights at another church in town.

The drive to the church was across town, giving me ample time to consider turning around. Something, or rather Someone, kept guiding me to keep driving. I channel surfed on the radio for several minutes, finally letting the dial rest on a song, "Calling All Angels," sung by the musical group, Train. The message of the music spoke to my soul. As I listened to the lyrics in the song, I had this overwhelming feeling that something or someone from "that March night" would be there. Someone, an angel, so-to-speak, to guide me toward the next step of my journey. Chills filled me. The hair on my arms stood at attention. God was at work, and I could feel His presence, His provision.

The sanctuary was full with more than three hundred ladies in attendance. As they sang in unison, their high and sweet-sounding voices echoed off the church walls. It was loud. It was compelling to hear. I took a seat in the back, as I was one of the new faces, which left its own insecurities with me. *Is this where God wants me to be?* Still struggling with the guilt of spending my evening away from Ayden after being gone all day at work, my eyes fought the tears of knowing my son was home asking where Mommy went. I allowed this feeling to cause doubt in my mind that this is where God had directed me. However, as the evening progressed, that doubt was quickly dismissed through the events, the signs, God gave me to know I was exactly where He wanted me to be.

Sarah stood in the front of the church in her freshly pressed suit. She explained the history of BSF, how it was started many years ago for the purpose of offering an intimate Bible study for women all over the world. It was a way to get to know the Lord at a much deeper level, among women who shared the same thirsting. After the introductions were made, she asked that the group discussion leaders meet in their assigned classrooms with the other members of their classes. They spent the next thirty minutes discussing the Acts of the Apostles at an in-depth and intimate level. As they funneled out of the sanctuary, Sarah asked that the new gals attending stay in the sanctuary for an introduction class.

I sat among twelve women who, like me, had never been to BSF before. We learned more about the history, filled out paperwork to register for the class, and met the other staff members. At this point, I was not yet hooked on the whole concept, still thinking about my husband and son whom I had left at home. But I respectfully sat and listened.

The half hour passed, and all the women began to saturate the sanctuary again. I watched them as they made their way through the white double doors. I still had the feeling God would reconnect me with someone from that March 4 night.

She entered through the back door of the sanctuary. My glance at her became a stare followed by overwhelming, chilling sense. Confusion, fear, and excitement set in. Her eyes met mine. She approached me from the front of the sanctuary. I felt my pulse rising.

She smiled. "How are you?" she asked.

"I'm doing well; how are you?"

It was Susan Ritter, the former hospital administrator. The police had awakened her late in the evening on the night Christopher had died. She was all too familiar with the events that unfolded.

I wasn't sure where God was taking me. Still guarded from the scrutiny of the trial, I continued to proceed cautiously. We had not seen each other in more than seven years and now, during my time of fervently seeking the Lord's direction, our paths had crossed. We chatted for a few moments about the changes we had made over the past seven years. I told her about my journey since the trial; about my faith, my marriage to Dale, his boys, Ayden, and life in general. Our casual conversation quickly became distinct and purposeful.

"Do you remember "Janet Martin"?" she asked.

"I think so. She was a nurse on the adult unit, right?" I asked.

"Yes. She works at "Lindley Hospital" now, and would you believe that her coworkers are *still* talking about that March night?"

A knot swelled in my throat. "Are they talking about it in a good way?"

She exclaimed, "No! A negative way."

I briefly mentioned my thoughts about God being "up to something" and that I had started writing a book about it many years ago. I continued. "Recently, I've felt this overwhelming urge to continue writing about it, to share how God has used it for good despite all the pain. But I get *so scared* when I think about it. How will everyone respond? The family? The other people involved?"

Our conversation was instantly interrupted with the high-pitched singing through the voices surrounding us.

"I'll talk to you later," she whispered.

The worship service began, and I listened intently. The anger and fear of the event began to creep back into my mind as my blood pressure climbed.

Two hymns later, Sarah opened with a prayer. She asked God for His presence, as this lesson dealt with fear, the fears and doubts that we face when God is beginning something new. I couldn't believe what I was hearing as I sat in my own pool of fear. She continued praying. My mind continued racing. I had been dismissing God's signs for months, chalking it up to "coincidences" or just "a crazy idea." Maybe you can relate. We minimize the power He has over our lives; I kept thinking He couldn't possibly be calling *me* to do His work.

I was overwhelmed. God was using Sarah to look right into my soul and speak to my fears. She opened her Bible and asked us to turn to Ephesians 6:19–20, and she read, "Pray also for me, that whenever I open my mouth, words may be given me so that I will fearlessly make known the mystery of the gospel, for which I am an ambassador in chains. Pray that I may declare it fearlessly, as I should."

The hair on my arms rose even higher, as I felt heaven's nudge.

Her message continued with this little tidbit of reflection and wisdom. "When God gives us knowledge and wisdom of His word, promises and assignments, we will be greeted with opposition. But as Scripture has promised, we are armed with his love and protection to spread his teachings."

My responsibilities became all too clear through this sermon. Suddenly, the three hundred other women were no longer on my radar. My focus rested solely on how this stranger standing before me was telling me *exactly* what God wanted me to hear. *Okay! Okay! I get it, God. Now how do I proceed?*

In His gentle and quiet voice, God spoke, "Follow me."

After the service concluded, Susan and I revisited. She looked at me and said as plain as white bread, "That message was for you."

"I know, I know," I responded.

She smiled and said, "Your work is not over, Megan."

God used March 4, 1998, and all the agony after it to better my life by making a believer out of me and now He was calling me to share this fantastic news, the message of hope that only He could orchestrate.

My cup, the one that had been so empty for so many years, began to refill. As I walked out of the church that night, God's provision and sovereignty was so real, so tangible. God put Susan and Sarah, His angels, in my path to guide me. The drive home was different. I felt a sense of peace building in me, a peace I had not encountered, consistently, for more than seven years.

My husband greeted me when I arrived home. I hugged him, checked on my son who lay fast asleep in bed, and sat down to reflect.

"How was it?" Dale asked.

I could only reply, "God is really talking to me."

Simple yet to the point, he replied, "Well, are you listening?" Dale had been pushing me to "just write the book" for months. He tried to convince me it could only foster good things.

I replied, "Yes, I finally have an answer to my long-awaited prayer, and I'm definitely listening." Through this journey I have discovered that when God speaks, he doesn't care if it is our bedtime; we need to listen.

That night I lay in bed, watching the clock. My mind replayed the events of the evening. My thoughts seemed to overflow and talk to me, just like that computerized voice on the GPS. The instruction replayed over and over again. "Then he said to them all: Whoever wants to be my disciple must deny themselves and take up their cross daily and *follow me*" (Luke 9:23, NIV, emphasis added).

Follow me, Meg. Follow me.

After hours of lying awake, I prayed and asked God to let me rest for the evening. I knew the demand of daily life would soon be approaching with a six thirty chime. I fell asleep somewhere around three a.m.

The alarm sounded. I peeled myself out of bed, showered, dressed, and drank my first of many cups of coffee. The demands of motherhood set in for the day as I dressed my son, dressed myself, pinned my hair atop my head, grabbed makeup bag in hand, and headed out the door. We arrived at his daycare, said our good-byes for the day, and headed into our routines.

Suddenly I was consumed with an idea, a direction. *I'll stop by the local bagel shop and grab a bag of bagels for everyone in the office.* I never do things like this unless we are celebrating a co-worker's birthday or some other special occasion. I sat inside my minivan for two minutes of primping with mascara and lipstick and then quickly hurried inside. Although I barely noticed the presence of others around me, hers hit me like a ton of bricks. Nurse Janet, the same nurse Susan had just told me about the night before, was sitting at a table in the bagel shop with a friend.

I stood speechless.

I gathered myself to remember why I was there—bagels. I grabbed a baker's dozen and headed to the counter. As I stood in line waiting to pay, I overheard Janet talking with her companion about her coworkers and how she wanted a new job—one away from the past, where people would stop talking "about that night." She looked so sad, so stressed, and so empty. I could relate.

Again, I stood with chills.

I debated. *Do I approach her? What do I say? Should I ask questions?* Not knowing how to respond, I left without saying a word to her. God had already spoken to me through her presence, another sign of reassurance that I was on the right track—His track. He had guided me here and had spoken to my heart. I knew He was leading me down the road to tell my story—His story of *grace, mercy, and hope.* To share the good that came after a very bad situation. During the days of the trial, I never would have imagined or understood how God could use this story for good. But He has and still is. Through God's Provision and Sovereignty (GPS), He guided me to do just that.

"Trust in the Lord with all your heart, and lean not unto your own understanding. In all your ways, acknowledge Him, and He will direct your path" (Proverbs 3:5–6, NIV).

CHAPTER 16

Happy Father's Day

I vividly remember our first date. During the course of our three-hour conversation, Dale said, "I want a daughter." I sat at our restaurant table thinking; *Well, you're not getting one tonight, buddy!*

Dale's passion and desire for a little girl was infectious. After having two boys from his previous marriage, he was ready to get a dose of baby estrogen. Years later, after marriage and the birth of our son Ayden, Dale and I began talking about having one more child. Since my childhood, I had always envisioned my future with two children; one of each would be ideal. I realized Dale's history of producing boys probably left the odds for "one of each" pretty slim. I was okay with that. I just truly wanted to birth two healthy children. Dale was a little unsure about having another child. As we all do, he kept finding all the reasons not to—age, finances, time—when the Lord was showing *me* all the reason *to* have another baby.

After months of our struggle to get on the same page, and many empty attempts on my part to convince him about what the Lord had laid on my heart, I let go of it and gave it back to Him. I prayed, through many nights of tears, that if this was God's will, He would give Dale a desire for another child. And I prayed that if another child was not in His will, I asked him to take the desire *out* of my heart.

A few weeks went by, and I held my tongue, all the while yearning so much inside for another child, a new life to grow and nurture. I slowly began to see God at work with Dale. Dale started pointing out other babies in restaurants and stores, how cute and lovable they were. The glimmer in his eyes that I remembered from our first date began to sparkle once again. God was turning him, gently and slowly, away from fears and excuses toward the desire for a baby. I continued to hold back and just watch Him work.

On October 23, 2006, I woke expecting my monthly visit from the estrogen fairy. Nothing. My first (guarded) reaction was "it's just late." I guarded myself against another month of a pregnancy test I was sure was going to be negative. After showering and dressing for work, I decided to put my skeptical and cynical mind to rest and thought, *I'll take a test.* Dale had already left for work, so I knew he wouldn't see the test and wouldn't prompt the discussion, and debate, again.

I did the "deed" and left the test in the bathroom while I ventured to the kitchen for a quick morning bite. Moments later, I returned to the bathroom. I glanced down at the counter—

only to find two lines! *Can this really be? Am I really pregnant?* My excitement grew, though my skepticism kept me somewhat guarded against the possibility of a "dud test." It's amazing how powerful doubt can be sometimes. And I know the source of it is not God, but Satan.

He constantly offers doubt when God is clearly at work.

I was headed out of town that morning on an overnight trip for work. Mom and Ayden were tagging along for the scenic ride. Before I left, however, I had to (rather I convinced myself I had to) make a quick stop at the doctor's office for another test. There's that doubt again. I had to know what I had seen at home was real before I shared it with Dale. Part of me was still not sure what reaction I would face. Would he be happy? Had God really set things straight in his mind and in his heart? What would I do if He hadn't?

After checking in at the front desk, the nurse took me back to the lab. She gave me a pregnancy test and escorted me to the restroom. After I finished, I sat in the waiting room for the results, still in awe of what was happening.

She came out with a smile. "Yes, you're pregnant."

My smile resumed even bigger than before. That second confirmation truly sealed the deal. *Now I'm really pregnant.* Like I wasn't before the second test? *Thank you, God!* I was so excited! I hugged the nurse and left the office.

Mom and Ayden waited for me at home to make our departure on our overnight trip. I couldn't wait to tell Dale—but I would wait because I didn't want to share this kind of news over the phone. Holding this news from Dale made our trip feel like an eternity.

When we arrived home just two days later, I shared the news with Dale, while bracing myself for his reaction.

"Well how about that!" he exclaimed as the boyish sparkle returned to his eyes. He was so excited!

God *had* given Dale peace and comfort, and now we were going to have a baby!

Yes! Thank you, Lord!

The pregnancy progressed as normal. My twenty-week ultrasound was scheduled for February 14, Valentine's Day. Dale and I met at the doctor's office at 8:30 a.m. and waited for the technician to take us into the room. She took us back and set me up on the table. As she examined the baby through the scanner, we saw a healthy baby growing. Ten toes, ten fingers, beautiful profile, and lots of hair! She continued to scan the baby to determine the gender. Our feisty little one didn't seem to want to cooperate. After many diligent attempts to get a clear look at the bottom end of our baby, the technician finally got a clear shot. She looked at the three lines (girl) on the monitor, grinned at us, and said "There's the hamburger!" *As opposed to a hot dog?* I thought. I guess she needed a little catchphrase humor too. It didn't offend me though—God had granted us a little girl! I looked up at Dale with tears in my eyes, only to see him crying too. All our prayers—my prayer for another child, our prayer for a healthy baby, and Dale's prayer for a little girl—were answered in the glimpse of a monitor.

Thank you, Lord!

After my appointment, I headed back to the office. On my way I stopped the car and went inside the local florist. Now, keep in mind, it was around noon on Valentine's Day. The place was packed with people, mostly men, purchasing flowers, balloons and gift baskets. I walked up to the desk and asked the clerk if he had any pink roses. He looked at me like I was a purple alien from Mars. "No, I'm all out." I glanced over to my left and saw a sweet, cuddly pink teddy bear sitting on a shelf. "I'll take that and some pink carnations, please." I felt like I was floating on a cloud! Pure joy.

She was due on July 3. As my pregnancy moved along without complication, I once again felt a deepening with my relationship to the Lord. It's amazing how He uses children, born or unborn, to show us just how deep His love goes. Life is truly His miracle. Over several months during my early pregnancy, He began to speak to me about my commitment to Him and the need to display the level of depth in love that He had carried me to. Through Sunday morning services, daily devotions, and prayer, He really convicted me that it was necessary for me to take the next step in walking along the path He had set before me. Just as my growing belly was a display of a life developing within, baptism by immersion was the outward display of my spiritual life that had also grown to new measurements. As I absorbed this instruction, I felt I needed to truly understand what the difference was between what I had done—baptism by sprinkling—six years prior.

I consulted our associate pastor. During a one-on-one meeting with him, I shared what God had laid on my heart. I asked for his guidance. He walked me through Scripture to show me what God's word says in Matthew 3:16 about baptism: "And Jesus, when he was baptized, went up straightway out of the water: and, lo, the heavens were opened unto Him, and He saw the Spirit of God descending like a dove, and lighting upon him." He explained to me that in order to come "up straightway out of the water," Jesus had to first go under the water. He had to be completely immersed in the water, not just sprinkled by the water.

There it was. I needed to be immersed; that message became clear. I asked our associate pastor if he would baptize me.

"I'd be honored," he replied.

Then we discussed when. "The sooner, the better," I said.

We looked at the upcoming weekend. He was going to be out of town. "I can do it the following Sunday during the 9:30 a.m. service." The date? *March 4*, 2007.

Seriously.

I'm not kidding.

On the day of my immersion, I remember a brief moment of reflection, standing in awe of God's once again perfect timing. This day was not only a remarkable moment in my life but I had the added bonus of sharing it with my unborn daughter. As I stood in the water, waiting for the official dunking of my disappointments, disillusions, and doubts from the world, I found myself truly rejoicing and thanking God for his grace.

As an aside, I said to the pastor, looking down at my very large belly, "Do you think you'll be able to lift me back up?"

He smiled. "You and the baby will be fine."

With the exception of some serious heartburn—and I mean *serious*—all was fine until about the seventh month of my pregnancy. I felt a strong pull deep within my abdomen followed by what I thought was a rush of warm water inside. I told my doctor about it at my next checkup, and he immediately ordered an ultrasound. The ultrasound revealed several things. The umbilical cord appeared to be short and it wrapped behind her neck. And she was a *big* baby, already six pounds, ten ounces, with six weeks still remaining.

"We need to monitor you every week until she comes," the doctor said. He continued. "We'll need to do another C-section because of her size." He explained that short cords were common, but just to be safe, we needed to watch it closely for location and length. "If you feel a decrease in activity or a large increase in her activity, call us immediately."

We scheduled my ultrasound and non-stress test (NST) for the following week. A rush of fear came over my body.

I came home that night and shared the news with Dale. I was scared—we had both waited so long for our little girl, and now this?

"She'll be okay," Dale said.

I wanted to believe that, but it was just so scary. I wanted so badly to know, with certainty. Instead, I just had to *choose* to trust God. God had granted us this child, and I had to trust Him to keep her safe. I started the NSTs the following week and continued for the next three weeks. The reports were all good, but the uncertainty—the doubt—still lay in the back of my mind.

I was home on the Saturday before my scheduled C-section, just three days away. I had been working in the baby's room getting it ready for her arrival, stacking diapers in the changing table, organizing her pretty pink clothes while standing in awe of all the pretty pink blankets, pink bonnets, and pink booties. Once you've filled your home with boys and are now expecting a girl, there only needs to be one color in the crayon box: *pink*!

I guess I "nested" a little too much that day because I started feeling some pains I had never felt before. Pressure was building, and it felt like she was making her debut. Dale had taken Ayden with him to Mom's house to cut her grass. Since the time of Ayden's birth, Mom had moved to North Carolina and lived about eight miles down the road from us.

I was alone in our house. I lay on the couch, trying to catch my breath and remain calm. *What's happening?* It didn't feel the way I thought it was *supposed* to feel (whatever that means). It just felt different. I put a call in to the doctor's office and left a message with the nurse.

Moments later, the phone rang. It was my doctor. I was so relieved. "What's going on?" he asked.

"I feel pressure. It's tight and feels like she's falling out." I was scared.

He replied. "It sounds serious. Meet me at the hospital. Do you have a ride?"

Catching my breath, I replied, "Yes, I'll see you there in a little while."

I hung up and dialed Dale's cell. Voice mail. I called Mom's phone. Answering machine. I started panicking. I tried Dale's again. Voice mail. Then I called his son, Charlie's, cell phone, who was also with Dale. Voice mail. *Come on*! I thought. *He's a teenager for crying out loud—they never turn their cell phones off! This isn't happening!*

I called again and again. *I've got to get there.* My neighbor was out of town. *I'll drive myself.* I climbed into the car and headed out the driveway. My doctor would have read me the riot act if he knew what I was doing. I was desperate. I got to the end of our road and dialed Mom's number one more time. Finally she answered. "Mom! I need Dale to come get me and take me to the hospital! I think it's time. Send him home, *now!*" I hung up, turned the car around, and pulled back in the driveway. I burst into tears. I was scared. This was all happening so fast and I was alone.

Ten minutes later Dale pulled in our driveway with Mom following right behind in her car. Dale climbed out and headed toward our front door.

"What are you doing?" I pleaded.

"Let me just get a quick shower, I'm covered with grass."

"*What?* Get in the car *now!*" It wasn't a pretty sight, like a scene from a Friday afternoon soap opera scene that leaves you hanging until Monday's episode airs.

He hopped in the car as I looked up—my son, now four, stood

crying in the doorway with my mom. "Mommy, come back!" he screamed. It was awful. I still cry when I think about how it made Ayden feel, seeing me like that and not understanding what was happening.

This wasn't part of *our plan*.

We arrived at the hospital. I was greeted with a wheelchair and rolled back to the exam room. The fetal monitor confirmed that I was having contractions. The nurse called the doctor.

He came in and examined me. He paused, looked at the readout from the monitor, and looked up. "You're having contractions but no dilation yet. Well, you're here. You're three days away from your scheduled surgery. I've already called the OR. Let's do it."

I nearly gave myself whiplash as I turned to Dale, who sat on the opposite side of the bed. "I haven't seen you smile that big in nine months," he joked.

"We're going to have her tonight!" I squealed. I was so excited! She was finally going to be here—this journey of uncertainty was coming to an end, and we would know for sure that she was okay.

The entourage of doctors, nurses, and surgical techs rolled me to down to the OR. I was prepped, laid on the table, and we were underway. Molly Elizabeth was born on June 16, 2007, at 8:30 p.m. She was perfect—not a thing wrong. No cord issues. In fact, her cord was long and healthy. Her little cry was like music to our ears. And her color?

Perfectly *pink*, of course.

The nurses took her to be cleaned and weighed. I was in

recovery for about two hours. We finally got settled into our room a little after midnight on the third Sunday in June. Shortly after, the nurses brought her to us. Dale held her, and I looked up at him and then looked at the clock.

I looked back at Dale and said, "Happy Father's Day, honey." We both just cried in awe of God's *perfect timing* and our beautiful *gift*.

"Sons are a heritage from the Lord, children a gift from him" (Psalm 127:3).

CHAPTER 17

The Next Step

When our church bulletin listed the upcoming Living Proof Live conference at the RBC Center in Raleigh, I felt another gentle nudge by God. Beth Moore started this ministry in 1994. She explains in her literature that God called her to ministry work through writing. His specific instruction to her was to minister to women (http://www.lproof.org/).

My best friend, English, and I signed up for the conference in Raleigh. During the weeks that led up to the conference I prayed and prayed. I had gotten "stuck" in the process of writing this book and asked God to give me the next step. During my moments of pleading to Him for His guidance, I experienced this overwhelming feeling God was going to reveal the next step in this journey to me.

As we entered the arena, the vibrations and spiritual booming coming from the praise band were exhilarating. The ministry's impact was noticeable by the thousands of women who were already seated inside. We found our seats in the nosebleed section of the arena and joined in, singing to the music as it scrolled across the large TV screens. We clapped our hands and took notice of the surrounding ladies worshipping the Lord.

One half hour later, Beth Moore took the stage. She welcomed us and began her story of how God brought her to Raleigh to speak. She explained that she had been "instructed by God" about a month prior to her visit. She seemed intrigued by His message. God had given her a clear instruction to "step it up," "it" being the next step in our faith and walking another step closer to finding our purpose from the Lord. She explained He had repeatedly told her "the victory has already been won" in Raleigh. She giggled and said, "I have no idea what that means … but God kept telling me, 'The victory has already been won.'" She continued. "In all my twenty-four years of speaking, God has never given homework to the women I speak to—until now."

"Raleigh girls, when this weekend is over, you have some homework to do." God had instructed her with a specific Bible study for the "Raleigh girls." The songs of ascents begin at Psalm 120 and go through Psalm 134. She continued, "I have set up a study on my website, specifically for the women who have attended this conference." A password was given. She made one request: "After you have finished the fifteen-step study of 'The Songs of Ascent,' please write me a one-page letter and tell me *why* we are doing this—in other words, what has changed in your walk with Him. In her charming whit, she continued instructing. "If nothing has changed for you … don't write me."

The crowd erupted with laughter.

A chill set in across my body. During the hour ride to the conference, English and I had talked about our expectations. I told her, "I really feel as if God is going to use this to push me forward ... I've been praying about it for weeks."

Beth Moore was the messenger to this next step. God knew I would be attending this conference, as I had felt Him lead me to. I couldn't wait to see what God had in store for me.

The conference lasted through Saturday afternoon. English and I discussed the messages and how we felt changed. I returned home and wrote that Saturday night. I reflected on how, when God tells us to do something, we are not to let fear consume our lives. The material just began to flow. I was exhilarated at God's messages, and I couldn't seem to type fast enough.

Ten p.m. approached and fatigue set in. When God is hard at work in our lives, it takes a lot of energy. At some point that energy wanes so we can rest. And God honors our periods of rest—after all His creating, He too rested on the seventh day. I went to bed shortly after I finished another chapter, and I had planned to spend Sunday evening writing more.

Our evening routine with our son consisted of dinner, a bath, a bedtime story, a prayer, and then sleep. As I lay with Ayden while he drifted off to sleep, Dale sat on the couch in the living room watching TV.

He called me in and said, "Meg, you've gotta see this." He was watching a special news report. The reporter interviewed several parents in Texas who had put their children in psychiatric group facilities. Since 1985, fifteen children had died while being restrained, yet none of the caregivers involved had ever been criminally charged. The parents were irate, they were sad, but most of all they wanted someone to make this pattern stop. The reporter never interviewed anyone from the facility or anyone who was involved with the restraints. The only interviews that aired were of angry parents.

I sat still, feeling a swarm of emotions come over me. The fears of March 4 came charging back. Writing was quickly pushed back and dismissed with fear. The fear of scrutiny. The fear of asking the question, "What if?" My husband saw this fear and anger building inside me. He apologized for calling me into the living room to see this program. I told him I wish he hadn't shown it to me either ... doubt set in.

Maybe this book is a mistake; maybe God is telling me to let it sit in the past; maybe this book will only stir up hurt?

I shared my thoughts with Dale and he quickly responded. "Honey, this is the same thing you went through ... you didn't do anything wrong."

I immediately said, "They didn't either; otherwise they would have been charged. It doesn't matter anyway, the stories have the same ending—a dead child—and everybody wants an answer why."

That night, I lay awake with all the fear spinning in my mind. I was consumed with the images of crying parents. I was angered at the ignorance of the reporter to only share one side of the story. The fire to defend these allegations grew inside me. The last thought I remember having before I fell asleep that night was simple: if these kids had the true love of God in their lives, they wouldn't have been in the hospital.

The alarm sounded at 6:30 a.m. I fought going back to sleep. I felt exhausted, mostly emotionally. My dreams of the past seven years were vivid that night—the death, the trial, and the desperate need for a solution. I climbed out of bed and continued with the morning routine.

After leaving my son's daycare, I headed to work. I listen to the Christian radio station during my travels. A constant stream of songs seemed to play with a persistent message: *testimony.* I parked the car and headed into the office. After checking voice mail and e-mail, my mind still played that news special over and over. I logged on to the website that gives me "Our Daily Bread" (http://odb.org/) each day. It offers scriptural passages, a reflection, and how it applies to our lives. The click on the webpage struck my heart. August 1, 2005: "Take as directed" was the theme. Dr. Smiley was addressing the issue of medicine and pills. And then it hit me. Our society has grown so accustomed to popping pills to make us feel better we've forgotten how to function without them. Why are we so quick to swallow a little pill?

Simple. We want quick fixes.

We don't take the time out of our busy lives to just sit and get real about who we are, where we are in life and most importantly, how we can change. We are quick to swallow a pill to make ourselves feel better. The problem, however, is that we have to take dose after dose after dose. The medicine wears off, and then we're right back where we started—hurting, depressed, and unfulfilled. My thoughts consumed me. The images of parents crying on the news, the use of medication for problems that can't be fixed by a pill and my own journey of struggling led me to this thought.

Something has got to change.

CHAPTER 18

Not Just a Band-Aid

A fever, headache, sore throat, and an upset stomach all equate to a nasty illness, one that will leave you miserable and down for the count. When we are sick we tend to focus on the symptoms, seeking relief from the pain and suffering. We can take medicine to ease the pain or reduce the fever, but this only temporarily helps; it doesn't offer a permanent solution. Until we treat the source of the symptoms—the infection—we will continue to suffer from the symptoms.

Our spiritual lives are similar to our physical health in the respect that we can try our own ways to deal with the symptoms of our broken hearts and lives, but until we seek God's lasting healing, we will find ourselves spinning on a wheel like a hamster, going nowhere and exhausting ourselves in the process.

I watched Dad struggle with depression for years. I could not comprehend what was making him sad. He had a wonderful wife, three terrific children, a beautiful home, and food on the table.

Why then, did he cry? Why did he find it hard to smile? Why did he sleep so much? All these questions lingered in my mind for years, but I could not bring myself to go further than the surface of the symptoms. It wasn't until depression entered my world that I knew the feelings, thoughts, and emotions were deeper than the symptoms.

I have had broken bones, a broken heart, two C-sections, and of course, menstrual cramps! But none of this pain came close to the agony I encountered when I found myself struggling with depression. This same pain I could not understand witnessing in my father as a child became all too familiar to me as an adult. It was an ache within my *spirit*—a longing for true and complete wholeness and purpose. It was a heart condition. A hole. Something was missing. I wanted to regain the ability to move forward from my life-altering experience, and I simply did not know how to recapture the essence of who I was created to be and what I was put here to do. And when there is a hole, we desperately try to fill it with what we think will fill that void, to avoid the pain of a broken heart.

There are lots of escapes for people who deal with depression. Some eat more. Some eat less. Some drink. Some spend money they don't have. Some run four miles a day, some lie in their bed from dawn until dusk. However, it seems as though whatever habit, pill, or activity we turn to, we usually forget the first place to look for help: our heavenly Father. Throughout my life and yours, He has been there. We have just shut Him out or ignored His presence. Fortunately, some people finally learn to turn to

God for answers, and then others continue to seek something entirely different -drinking, drugs, eating, binging, shopping, gambling, busyness - it doesn't matter what the addiction is, the root is always the same. There is a void and until that emptiness is filled with Christ, it will never be whole.

Dad turned to alcohol. He was not a violent person when he drank. He drank to sleep, and he slept to avoid his pain. And this cycle led to an even more detrimental issue: addiction. What began as a simple drink to "take the edge off" quickly turned into a vicious dependency.

My "out" was not eating much food and living a life at the gym. I thought maybe if I *look* better, I would *feel* better. Not so. When that didn't work, I turned to other escape routes. Among the list: therapy, antidepressants, drinking, busyness, and more therapy. I found that although these escapes were a quick fix, they didn't eliminate the cloud of bitterness, fear, and worry from my mind.

They didn't treat the *source* of the infection.

Many psychiatrists think medicine is the answer. Maybe it is for some. If a chemical imbalance is to blame for the dreary mood, then by all means, medicate. But if the source of the sadness isn't a matter of balancing the chemical scale, there's a deeper problem; the depth cannot be reached by simply treating the symptoms.

In my own experience dealing with depression, the issue wasn't chemicals. You can name an anti-depressant and I'm sure I've tried it. None of them reached the core of the issue; they simply numbed my reality and made me so tired I didn't have the energy to be sad. Occasionally, I found one that gave me a "boost," but the only impact it had on my day-to-day life was a cleaner house, freshly cut yard, and two hours of sweat at the gym. And after the jolt wore off, I found myself right back where I started.

Low.

Many psychologists think that if we talk about our feelings, we will find the wisdom to understand our illness. I have tried that too. Though it gave me insight as to the issues I carried in my emotional backpack, it didn't really help me put them down and let go of them, to restore balance in my life and experience true freedom from depression.

I am not trying to belittle either of these theories. They may work for some. But what about the higher percentage of our population those medications don't help? Do we sit back and say, "We tried"? Do we accept this as something that cannot be treated? That is not good enough. We as humans are too smart, curious, and eager to learn to just stop there.

Those approaches, alone, were unsuccessful in the long term. Simply popping a pill or conversing with a counselor every Wednesday wasn't a permanent solution for me to really get to the depths of my pain (the infection), and to heal from it. My communication needs to be daily, with God. Praying, seeking, listening, pleading with Him to relieve and release the hurt I was carrying.

Every. Day.

Think about that. Have you ever tried to lose weight by getting on a treadmill one time? Were you successful? Probably not. If you were successful, did the change in your pant size last beyond a week? Probably not. It requires intentional effort and daily work to maintain. The same is true for our spiritual transformations. It requires work, daily.

"If anyone would *come after me*, let him deny himself and take up his cross *daily* and follow me" (Luke 9:23, NIV, emphasis added).

Through the strength of the Holy Spirit within us, we can do the work. But, we have to get on the spiritual treadmill. And we have to do it every day. One of my prayers through sharing this story is that this book touches lives, changes thoughts on "treatment," and leads others to the true Source for healing. Depression and mental illness is everywhere in our world.

So is God.

With the power of prayer, we can start finding those things in our lives that really make our heart tick, without medication to give it a jump start. Seeking Christ, accepting Him into our hearts and lives and discovering our God-given purpose, what truly makes us tick, is the prescription for true healing and peace ... not the car we drive, the wallet we strive to stuff, the gray roots we color, or the bottle we drink from. God will fulfill our needs and give us the wholeness and peace that we so long for. Let's seek, crave, and drink Him. His power is everywhere, in abundance.

Overflowing. We just have to choose to tap into it.

"God has poured out his love into our hearts by the Holy Spirit, whom he has given us" (Romans 5:5, NIV).

CHAPTER 19

I Have a Brown Thumb

despise gardening. The whole process is, in my opinion, a pain. Bending over to pull weeds strains my already hurting lower back. Digging holes in North Carolina red-clay soil, among the numerous rocks, is frustrating. Planting bushes and flowers, only to have to constantly fertilize and water them, is time consuming. And did I mention the mosquitoes? I can't go outside in the spring or fall for more than a minute without those pesky things thinking I'm their dinner. But there's one type of plant that's worth the cost of the pain and suffering. Okay, maybe that phrase is a little bit of an exaggeration. Annoying is a better word; the whole process of gardening is annoying, to me. But, I'll do it.

For mums.

I love mums! They are so pretty, enriched with colors varying from white, golden yellow, vibrant orange, pretty pink, purple, and bold burgundy. And (the best part) they come back each year. I don't have to start the entire process of planting over and over and over again. With each passing year, they get bigger and more vibrant than the year before. There's just one catch. You have to prune them in order for the new buds to grow each summer.

When we moved in to a new house about four years ago, I planted several mums in my yard during the late part of the summer. They were pretty small. Over the course of several weeks after the initial planting, I spent time fertilizing and watering them. Once they were on their way to growing, I sat on my front porch just enjoying their beauty. It was worth all the effort, time, fertilizing, watering, and yes, mosquito bites, that I had endured.

After the first autumn frost, however, they died. As a result of the cold temperatures and shift in climate, their young, colorful buds quickly became dark, dried out, and brittle. They needed to be pruned. That was the only way they could grow back next summer. So I cut off the branches where they had become brittle and inflexible. After I pruned, I covered each mum with pine needles to protect the remainder of the mum from the cold winter elements. The only reason I knew how to care for these plants was because I read the "caring for" instructions that were tied to the plants when I bought them. By reading the instructions, I learned this was part of the process of nurturing them so next season, when the warmer weather came back, they would have a chance at surviving and blooming again. As a result of all of my efforts, the next season they not only came back to life, the mums were bigger, fuller, and even more vibrant than the year I first planted them.

So is the process of our faith.

When I first made the choice to accept Jesus as my Savior, I admittedly did not fully understand the depth of what that decision entailed. I knew I was a sinner in need of forgiveness. I knew Jesus had died on the cross for the sins of the world; for my sins. I knew I had asked Him to forgive me for my sins, and at the moment I said that prayer, He became my Savior. I knew a lot *about Jesus:* the songs from church, the stories in the Bible. But knowing *about* Him is not the same as *knowing Him.*

In order to really know Him, it meant I had to spend time—intentional time—developing a relationship with Him. Reading His Word, His "caring for" book, listening to His Word, hearing His "still, small voice"—the one that speaks so gently to my soul, and talking to Him. Only through the process of getting to know Him could He begin the process of pruning.

Pruning. It's painful. We don't like someone pointing things out about us that we need to let go of or change. We hold on to things for different reasons. Maybe it's comfortable. "I know that it's not right, but that's just the way I am." Maybe it's just what we want, our plan, on our terms, on our watch. Maybe we don't like feeling judged or disagreed with.

You agree with me, *right?*

On March 4, 2001 (the day I accepted Jesus as my Savior), I didn't know about the pruning process. I didn't understand that my newly seeded faith, just like the mums, would require intentional work. The seed of faith needed nurturing, by the right hands, in order to grow and produce beautiful, healthy buds.

And like those new mums, I was a young Christian in need of pruning. Admittedly, my old approach to life had a lot of dead branches. As the years progressed, God started cutting thoughts and behaviors off in me that were limiting my growth in Him, just like those dead branches on the mums were limiting new flowers from sprouting. My dead branches were branches of bitterness and unforgiveness.

Dr. Shann Ray Ferch, a psychologist who has studied this issue in depth, defines forgiveness as the ability "to cease to feel angry or resentful towards someone or something" (*Journal of Counseling and Development*, 1998, 261). When a person feels he or she has been wronged or someone has crossed a psychological, physical, or spiritual boundary, resentment, mistrust, and unforgiveness can occur. Over time, these feelings can build to a point that may seem irreversible. As many counselors have discovered over the years of working with clients on this topic, there seems to be "no easy way for clients to cease feeling such emotions" (Ferch, 1998, 261).

And they are correct.

Forgiveness doesn't come easily or naturally. As humans, we want to hold others accountable. As Americans, our judicial system fosters the belief that someone should be held responsible for any wrong he or she does; a penalty should be implemented. Time spent behind bars, money paid. I've never seen a guilty defendant set free just because the judge or jury was *feeling* forgiving that day. In many cases, particularly in families, unforgiveness about past events are held in grudges. For years. That's what I witnessed in my family. And, as many children do, I followed in those ugly footsteps after my trial. I was angry and bitter, mostly at the DA, who had allowed the case to be presented to the Grand Jury. *He could have stopped this.* I thought. There the seed of my bitterness took root in my heart. And God is clear about His position on bitterness. "See to it that no one misses the grace of God and that no bitter root grows up to cause trouble and defile many"(Hebrews 12:15, NIV).

Dr. Ferch adds the theological components to forgiveness. Theologians view forgiveness as an "opportunity for reconciliation or renewed harmony between God and self or between self and others" (Ferch, 1998, 261). Don't miss that part: "renewed harmony between God and self." Harmony. That's something I was lacking for years following my acquittal. My days were filled with depression and anxiety. Those emotions grew physical roots too. Many nights I spent grinding my teeth while I slept, when I was able to sleep. My mornings were consumed with an upset stomach because I faced another day of anxious thoughts and a bitter attitude. Forgiveness doesn't limit itself to the mind; it affects all areas. Just like the mums. If you don't cut off the dead branches, it will eventually kill the root of the plant. Forgiveness is a major factor to obtaining a healthy lifestyle. And in an effort to restore health and harmony in my life, God has taught me a lot about what forgiveness is and what it isn't.

Forgiveness isn't about the person who wronged you or about what they did or didn't do. Really, it isn't. I used to think it was. I used to think that if I forgave someone, somehow I was sending the message that what they did was okay. When Jesus forgave you, the message wasn't that your sins were acceptable to Him, but that your sins were forgiven *by Him*.

I also believed that if I forgave another person, somehow that made me weak. And, by golly, I was not going to be a wimp. Forgiveness takes strength, and a big dose of it. On our own, we don't have that amount of strength. We just don't. But it truly is in our weakness where God's strength shines. "That is why, for Christ's sake, I delight in weaknesses, in insults, in hardships, in persecutions, in difficulties. For when I am weak, then [He is] strong" (2 Corinthians 12:10, NIV). After years of wrestling with this issue, God has shown me what forgiveness really is.

Forgiveness is about *my* relationship with God, and it's about *your* relationship with Him too. Think about it. He forgave you and you didn't deserve it. He made the choice to take away your sins. Forever. He offered forgiveness when you didn't do a single thing to deserve it. He turned the key to open the door of bondage that those sins held you in so that you could live freely again, under His grace. And do you really think He did that because it felt good?

Beaten. Bleeding. Bruised. Thorns in His forehead. Nails in His hands.

Felt good? Really?

That was His *choice*—for you—to offer forgiveness so you can have a restored relationship with your heavenly Father. "Bear with each other and forgive one another if any of you has a grievance against someone. Forgive as the Lord forgave you" (Colossians

3:13, NIV). Reaching true forgiveness is difficult. We cannot accomplish it on our own strength. We need help to make the choice to forgive.

Thank God, He is that help.

God, in His gentle way, showed me how my unforgiveness was affecting the other areas of my life. I tried to cope with it on my own strength through dieting, excessive exercise, therapy, drinking, and medicine. But when He calls us to "cut off every branch in me that bears no fruit," He wants us to make a clean cut, not just cope. The only way I was able to make the break was through His assistance. He helped me by cutting the branches of bitterness, resentment, unforgiveness, and grudges. And when I finally chose to forgive, He lifted the load I had carried for far too long. The depression seized. The anxiety was gone. I felt anew once again. And although the pruning process was time consuming and yes, painful, it was, in my opinion, worth the flower of a brand new Meg.

"He cuts off every branch in me that bears no fruit, while every branch that does bear fruit he prunes so that it will be even more fruitful" (John 5:2, NIV).

CHAPTER 20

Reflections of the Ascent

God gave Beth Moore specific instructions for the "Raleigh Girls." Following the conclusion of the conference, she told us to read, study, reflect, and communicate with Him regarding Psalm 120–134. Beth explained she wasn't quite sure what the purpose of this "homework" was, but she felt sure this was coming from God.

On Monday afternoon following the conference, I knelled down, lowered my head in prayer and "took my place on my face," as Beth instructed us. Taking our place on the floor requires vulnerability and humility. When we are vulnerable, we are more accessible by God. She said humility to God is powerful. I prayed to God to show me His message through the first psalm. I felt certain God was going to drastically and clearly take my relationship with Him to the next step, to go deeper. I decided to incorporate this part of my journey with the Lord into a daily journal. Just one disclosure: I am not a theologian, so these passages are not an interpretation but my own personal reflections about how they spoke to me.

Psalm 120, NIV: "I call on the LORD in my distress, and he answers me. Save me, O LORD, from the lying lips and from deceitful tongues. What will he do to you, and what more besides, O deceitful tongue? He will punish you with a warrior's sharp arrows, with burning coals of the broom tree. Woe to me that I dwell in Meshech, that I live among the tents of Kedar! Too long have I lived among those who hate peace. I am a man of peace; but when I speak, they are for war."

My reflection: Prior to the criminal charge and then the trial, I was not a Christian, nor was I active in God's Word. I was lost. Depression had consumed me. I was scared. I needed help. The scrutiny of this death was everywhere, in the news and in my head; it burdened my heart. The sequence of events of March 4 played over and over again in my head. It was as though I was reliving the experience with every breath. The reporters found their latest story, this story, and they weren't letting it go. They seemed to thrive on the "what ifs," the "who did what," "who was going to jail," and for "how long." They had no conscience about them; they told the story so it would sell. They completely disregarded the lives this death touched. In my eyes, they were the enemy. Their lying lips and deceitful tongues were more challenging to deal with at times than the actual trial itself. I could not comprehend how a person could make a living trying to destroy another's life. If words alone could kill, I would not have survived this trial. Their words would have put me in my grave.

Psalm 121: "I lift up my eyes to the hills—where does my help come from? My help comes from the Lord, the Maker of heaven and Earth. He will not let your foot slip—He who watches over you will not slumber; indeed, He who watches over Israel will neither slumber nor sleep. The LORD watches over you—the LORD is your shade at your right hand; the sun will not harm you by day, nor the moon by night. The LORD will keep you from all harm—He will watch over your life; the LORD will watch over your coming and going both now and forevermore.

My reflection: Motherhood is amazing. It's so full of excitement, anticipation of all "the firsts," and of course it carries a lot of worry with it as well. Before I had kids, I could sleep for upward of twelve hours without realizing there even was a world around me. Now? Forget it. I can't remember the last time I got eight straight hours. Even if my kids sleep well, I'm up with every little sound. Any slight peep from either of them and I'm sitting up in bed like a foghorn just blew. When it comes to my kids' safety and well-being, I'm on guard 24/7.

God is the same way with all His children. He never sleeps. He is always watching out for our best interest and keeping the enemy at bay. He uses other people in our lives to do the same, especially during our moments of crisis or weakness.

I remember feeling a sense that everything would be okay at the end of the trial. I *knew from the core of my being* that I hadn't done anything wrong that March night; I'd only been trying to help. My brother, however, wasn't so certain the outcome of the trial would be favorable to me.

Since my father's passing, Jason had become extremely protective of me. He had become my shield. He was filled with worry; he carried enough concern for both of us. That worry kept him from sleeping at night. He watched over me during the week of the trial. On the day of my testimony, I was questioned by my own attorneys for almost two hours. Testifying left me weak but most of all, empty. I finally let it all out—the facts, the feelings, and the fears. As I stepped off the stand, Jason stepped up to take my hand. I grabbed on to him and immediately fell into his arms. I wept and he held me tightly. God had equipped Jason with the strength I desperately needed.

Over the course of the years following this time in my life, Jason and I have become even closer. My family traveled to Germany in November 2004 to spend a week with him and his family while they were stationed there with the United States Army. During a drive along Germany's gorgeous countryside, I remember a conversation with him. I told him how I felt emptiness in my life. I was frustrated and unfulfilled with my career, and I didn't feel as though I had accomplished anything of significance. Yes, I had wonderful fulfilling things in my life—my husband, a child, and a stable career. But I still felt there was more to life than that—the "it" factor: passion. I wanted the passion back. The passion I had when I worked at the hospital. Though I tried so desperately to subdue it, the passion to help others still sat within my soul. I wrestled for years to just let it go. But I couldn't, and God wouldn't let it go.

When I began to truly seek God's purpose behind keeping

this journey fresh and vibrant in my mind, I repeatedly asked Him, What do I do? He faithfully began revealing it to me. Talk, write, and *testify*. Testify. The vow I made to myself on the day the trial ended—the vow to "never tell this story again"—He would surely break. His vow for my life was just the opposite: keep talking, sharing, and testifying. This calling to write and speak about this event soon turned into a focus on how tragedy can be used for good—the *good* is sharing the hope for others to hear, to encourage them along whatever trial they are facing, to know there is light at the end of the tunnel (and it's not the headlight of an oncoming train).

Naturally this was something I discussed with family and friends. Jason's response was quite different from what I had anticipated. I thought he would tell me to "just let it go" and put it behind me, knowing how difficult and painful it was for me. But he surprised me. "I've seen this in you for a long time, sis. You've always wanted to help people. Go for it." God used Jason to watch over me then and He continues to stand by and encourage me now.

Psalm 122: "I rejoice with those who said to me, 'Let us go to the house of the LORD.' Our feet are standing in your gates, O Jerusalem. Jerusalem is built like a city that is closely compacted together, that is where the tribes go up, the tribes of the LORD, to praise the name of the LORD according to the statute given to Israel. There the thrones for judgment stand, the thrones of the house of David. Pray for the peace of Jerusalem: 'May there be peace within your walls and security within your citadels.' For the sake of my brothers and friends, I will say, 'Peace be within you.' For the sake of the house of the LORD our God, I will seek your prosperity.'"

My reflection:

Seeking God's will for my life began in the church, by reading and knowing His Word. Dale and I were very involved with our Sunday school class. I sat there, each Sunday morning, feeling thirsty. I thirsted for more of God's Word. I was intrigued by the Scripture, by the personal reflection, and by the input from the other class members. I wanted to know more. This desire began to build over the course of many months—years actually.

Other believers, friends, and family members continued to "check in" with me during the week. They were my encouragement, my sounding board, and "my tribe". They saw this passion for the Lord in me growing. It was evident God was taking me "somewhere" … the journey was just beginning to reveal itself, and my friends were as eager as I was to watch it unfold. We continued to pray that God would clearly and loudly direct me in His will. There was an overwhelming feeling of peace building in my soul. I knew, deep down in my soul, that this peace was the calm before God's storm in my life.

A storm of change, transformation, and a wave that would spread hope.

For many years following the trial, I felt stuck in a rut of depression, insecurity, and the fear of continuous scrutiny. Many people who saw me in public would tell me, "You look really familiar." I never knew how to respond. I always just assumed they knew my face from the news. In my mind, I thought that would be my identity forever.

I remember one specific incident. I scheduled an appointment with a doctor regarding my horrific seasonal allergies. Shortly after I checked in with the receptionist, the nurse came in the waiting room, called my first name, and escorted me back to the exam room. As she flipped through the pages of my medical record, she stopped. She glanced up at me, with a deer-in-the-headlight look on her face, and asked, "Are you the girl from the mental health hospital?"

I felt like this was going to follow me for the rest of my life. I just wanted to crawl in a hole and forget it. It seemed as though whatever I said to "defend" myself would be taken out of context and used against me, even years after the trial had concluded. So I stayed silent. Though the love of helping others still burned within me, I vowed I would never expose myself to that environment again.

I allowed my fear of persecution control my actions.

However, as time moved on, I began to realize God wasn't going to let me "just forget it and move on." He would show me how He was going to use this event for His glory. I really began to feel His calling on my life. There was "a hopeful ending" to this terrible tragedy and He was calling me to speak about it, to speak about the glorious light He had become in my life.

The amount of energy God put into His calling on my life, I resisted with the same force. As you can see through this book, He eventually prevailed. Once I could get past the fear, the excitement to spread His message grew like an out-of-control wildfire. He wouldn't let it cease. He woke me in the middle of the night with messages to share. Many times I tried to roll over and go back to sleep. He wouldn't let me. If I just got out of bed and wrote down the message, I could find the peace to go right back into a deep sleep.

He *pursues* those He has called.

Over months of this constant presence, He continued to flood me with ideas. In different ways and in different environments, He showed me how this message relates to many lives, not just one demographic or age. I wanted to tell all. I wanted them to know God can save us, shield us, protect us, direct us and reveal His will for our lives. We do not need to turn to destructive actions to deal with our problems. We can take it, all of it, to God. I felt a spiritual warfare building inside me. I looked up to God for help and direction.

Psalm 123: "I lift up my eyes to You, to you whose throne is in heaven. As the eyes of slaves look to the hand of their master, as the eyes of a maid look to the hand of her mistress, so our eyes look to the LORD our God, till He shows us his mercy. Have mercy on us, O LORD, have mercy on us, for we have endured much contempt. We have endured much ridicule from the proud, much contempt from the arrogant."

My reflection: God had mercy on me. He allowed the trial to happen for the purpose of reaching me; of saving me from not only contempt in a courtroom, but from the condemnation of my sins. He knew the outcome, but He had to let me hit rock bottom. That's the only way I would have known to look up. And, more importantly, to step up and into His will. I believe that the agendas of those that accused me of this have probably learned and grown as people and professionals. I don't know, but I certainly pray that they did. I know I did.

Psalm 124: "If the LORD had not been on our side—if the LORD had not been on our side when men attacked us, when their anger flared against us, they would have swallowed us alive, the flood would have engulfed us, the torrent would have swept over us, the raging waters would have swept us away. Praise be to the LORD, who has not let us be torn by their teeth. We have escaped like a bird out of the fowler's snare; the snare has been broken, and we have escaped. Our help is in the name of the LORD, the Maker of heaven and earth."

My reflection: I don't know what I would have done if God hadn't been in control of the trial. I don't know how the jury would have voted if that one juror hadn't said "we need to pray about this." I don't know how I would have survived this nightmare without God's light shining through all of the darkness. But I do know one thing. I won't ever forget who brought me out of the "fowler's snare." I know Him and I thank Him.

Psalm 125: "Those who trust in the LORD are like Mount Zion, which cannot be shaken but endures forever. As the mountains surround Jerusalem, so the LORD surrounds his people both now and forevermore. The scepter of the wicked will not remain over the land allotted to the righteous, for then the righteous might use their hands to do evil. Do good, O LORD, to those who are good, to those who are upright in heart. But those who turn to crooked ways the LORD will banish with the evildoers. Peace be upon Israel."

My reflection: I trust God. He has shown me, time after time, that He is faithful and that His power can conquer all things. I cannot do anything without His strength. I want to do His work, the work He instructs me to do. If He wants me to tell others my story so they can come to know His love, strength, and grace, then I'll do it. If I can be one of His small lights in the world, then I want to be that bulb, to shine His light and tell others about the good news.

Psalm 126: "When the LORD brought back the captives to Zion, we were like men who dreamed. Our mouths were filled with laughter, our tongues with songs of joy. Then it was said among the nations, 'The LORD has done great things for them.' The LORD has done great things for us, and we are filled with joy. Restore our fortunes, O LORD, like streams in the Negev. Those who sow in tears will reap with songs of joy. He who goes out weeping, carrying seed to sow, will return with songs of joy, carrying sheaves with Him."

My reflection: There is no greater joy on this earth than knowing and relating to the love offered freely by God. It is simply awesome. It makes me giddy. It makes me want to sing, despite my lacking ability to hold a note. His love cannot be measured or packaged. It's too huge and all-consuming. It makes me feel like I can fly. It's better than a new house, car, or pair of shoes, and definitely better than a pill.

Simply put, nothing compares.

I have spent far too many years crying over my trial. I'm ready to wipe the tears so I can see clearly and follow the path God has set for me. I have a seed. The seed of hope. God gave me that. And now I want Him to plant it in your life and watch how He makes it grow into an all-consuming and wonderful harvest in your life.

Psalm 127: "Unless the LORD builds the house, its builders labor in vain. Unless the LORD watches over the city, the watchmen stand guard in vain. In vain you rise early and stay up late, toiling for food to eat—for He grants sleep to those He loves. Sons are a heritage from the LORD, children a reward from him. Like arrows in the hands of a warrior are sons born in one's youth. Blessed is the man whose quiver is full of them. They will not be put to shame when they contend with their enemies in the gate."

My reflection: When I started writing this book right after the trial ended, admittedly, it was out of bitterness. I wanted some kind of payment for the pain I went through: revenge, an apology, something to make the pain go away. But as the Lord has taught me, if we labor out of vain, it only brings more pain. Frustration. Hurt. Depression. Bitterness. My efforts went down the tube fast. Life got in the way and gave me less and less time to write. The demands and responsibilities of a new marriage, career, and children consumed my awake time, so I eventually just gave up on the idea of writing. However, after years of giving up on writing "my" story, God put His story in my heart to write about. The Lord has undoubtedly built this new ministry in my heart.

So now my efforts are not in vain, they are in love and in passion. The passion to follow His lead, and yes, to help others.

Psalm 128: "Blessed are all who fear the Lord, who walk in his ways. You will eat the fruit of your labor; blessings and prosperity will be yours. Your wife will like a fruitful vine within your house; your sons will be like olive shoots around your table. Thus is the man blessed who fears the LORD. May the LORD bless you from Zion all the days of your life; may you see the prosperity of Jerusalem, and may you live to see your children's children. Peace be upon Israel."

My reflection: I am scared to death to disappoint God, to miss out on His plan for my life, to miss the blessings He offers. That is the healthy fear associated with walking with the Lord. Not one of terror, but rather of true devotion to be in His will. There will come a time when I have to answer questions about what I did here on earth … and let me tell you, God won't like to hear, "I didn't have time" or "I was scared." That simply won't fly. Saying yes means putting on my big-girl work boots, picking up heaven's hammer, and getting a little dirty by doing the work He has appointed me to do.

I remember the overwhelming feeling of accomplishment at the end of each day I worked on a Habitat house. I was filthy, stinky, less than attractive, and I loved every minute of it. I had helped people, total strangers, get their feet back under themselves, get grounded and focused so they could pass the seed of hope to the next person in line.

Not only do I want this fulfillment for my own life, I want

my children to realize there are people in the world who need help and that we are God's servants. We must offer a helping hand to one of our brothers or sisters in Christ. He has put us here, given us abilities and talents that are supposed to be used for His glory, not ours. Our lives should never be so busy and filled with our own agendas, that we cannot answer His call. I want them to know that He reigns over all of us, and that includes our time. We should never be "too busy" or "too good" to get "too dirty." Hard work brings blessings; maybe not in monetary form as we tend to think but rather in joy knowing we have made a positive difference in someone else's life. Random acts of kindness seem to be fewer and fewer these days. And Dale and I want our children to know it doesn't have to be that way.

Psalm 129: "They have greatly oppressed me from my youth—let Israel say they have greatly oppressed me from my youth, but they have plowed my back and made their furrows long. But the LORD is righteous; he has cut me free from the cords of the wicked. May all who hate Zion be turned back in shame. May they be like grass on the roof, with it the reaper cannot fill his hands, nor the one who gathers fill his arms. May those who pass by not say, 'the blessing of the LORD be upon you; we bless you in the name of the LORD.'"

My reflection: After months of hearing my name on the news in a negative context, I was content to just fly so low in life that a radar detector couldn't find me. I felt like I had been pushed down to the point of no return. But God made it clear that although I had been at that point, He had a plan to bring me back up ...

and to bring me back up stronger and more equipped to fight the good fight. He brought me up to take the high road, His road. To bless those who cursed me or wronged me instead of retaliating out of bitterness and anguish.

Psalm 130-134: "Out of the depths I cry to you, O LORD; O LORD, hear my voice. Let your ears be attentive to my cry for mercy. If you, O LORD, kept a record of sins, O LORD, who could stand? But with You there is forgiveness; therefore You are feared. I wait for the LORD, my soul waits, and in His Word I put my hope. My soul waits for the LORD more than watchmen wait for the morning. O Israel, put your hope in the LORD, for with the LORD is unfailing love and with Him is full redemption. He Himself will redeem Israel from all their sins. My heart is not proud, O LORD, my eyes are not haughty; I do not concern myself with great matters or things too wonderful to me. But I have stilled and quieted my soul; like a weaned child with its mother; like a weaned child is my soul within me. O Israel, put your hope in the LORD both now and forevermore. O LORD, remember David and all the hardships he endured. He swore an oath to the LORD and made a vow to the Mighty One of Jacob: 'I will not enter my house or go to my bed—I will allow no sleep to my eyes, no slumber to my eyelids, till I find a place for the LORD, a dwelling for the Mighty One of Jacob.' We heard it in Ephrathah, we came upon it in the fields of Jaar. 'Let us go to his dwelling place; let us worship at his footstool—arise, O LORD, and come to your resting place, You and the ark of Your might. May Your priests be clothed with righteousness; may Your saints sing for joy.' For the sake of David Your servant, do not reject Your anointed one. The Lord swore an oath to David, a sure oath that He will not revoke: 'One of your own descendants I will place on your throne—if your sons keep my covenant and the statutes I teach them, then their sons will sit on your throne for ever and ever.' For the LORD has chosen Zion, He has desired it for his dwelling: 'This is my resting place for ever and ever; here I will sit enthroned, for I have desired it. I will bless her with abundant provisions; her poor will I satisfy with food. I will clothe her priests with salvation, and her saints will ever sing for joy. Here I will make a horn grow for David and set up a lamp for my anointed one. I will clothe his enemies with shame, but the crown on his head will be resplendent.' How good and pleasant it is when brothers live together in unity! It is like precious oil poured on the head, running down on the beard, running down on Aaron's beard, down upon the collar of his robes. It is as if the dew of Hermon were falling on Mount Zion. For there the LORD bestows his blessing, even life forevermore. Praise the LORD, all you servants of the LORD who minister by night in the house of the LORD. Lift up your hands in the sanctuary and praise the LORD. May the LORD, the Maker of heaven and earth, bless you from Zion."

My reflection:

I cried, and cried and cried. And He heard every tear hit the floor. Not only did He hear me, He offered mercy. And grace. And forgiveness. These passages reassure and reaffirm God's promises to me that He is my Redeemer, my forgiver, my hope, and my shelter. He will never leave my side; He is my warrior. He is my help. I know I can do anything with His blessing and will. He has called me to speak, write, and share His message; of that I am certain. I don't have to live in fear anymore.

O Lord! You've got my back. Thank you, Jesus!

As I sat reading, absorbing and reflecting on Psalm 120–134, I was in awe. God led Beth to lead me to these passages. He reaffirmed the trial, the fight, the obstacle of fear, the turning point into faith, the ministry He has set before me, and the fight "back" into His will for my life. I felt so energized. The adrenaline, once again, flooded my veins.

I am so incredibly humbled and blessed! Thank you, Lord!

And thank you, Beth. I'm sorry I didn't limit my letter to one page.

CHAPTER 21

The Greatest Love of All

In the mid-1980s, the late Whitney Houston sang "The Greatest Love of All", a song that directs one's attention to seek out true love, to find a hero to help guide us through life. Whenever I hear her strong, show-stopping voice sing this song on the '80s rock station, I get goose bumps.

As a child, my hero was my dad. Despite his addiction, I still looked up to him for strength, love and guidance. However, that all changed when he died. Though I could recall his catchy whimsical phrases, I could no longer seek his advice. As I walked through the years that followed, I was never more desperate for divine wisdom, guidance and strength.

Thank God, He became that for me.

We are all God's children, and He is our strength in love. He is our foundation. Are we building on what He has established, or are we trying to build our own empire? Even if we try to build our own empire, God has the power to make us leave it, knock it down, flip it over, and turn it into what He wants it to be. Deuteronomy 6:5–9 states we are to "Love the LORD your God with all your heart and with all your soul and with all your strength. These commandments that I give you today are to be upon your hearts. Impress them on your children. Talk about them when you sit at home and when you walk along the road, when you lie down and when you get up."

What are we teaching our children? Are we teaching them to love the Lord and depend on His strength? Or are we filling their lives with TV, videos games, and endless sporting events? Are we spending time with them, minus a TV, computer, or cell phone? Have our lives gotten so full of "stuff" and to-do lists that we can't even find time for a family meal together? Are we pumping them full of medicine to dissipate their energy?

The number of children who take medication to "fix" their problems is astounding. During my time at the hospital, I was simply disheartened by the medicine cabinets. I found my largest frustration in the fact that their problems were fixable with some good ole' TLC—the TLC that I now know is the True Love of Christ. Many of their environments were unstable: no set bedtimes, no square meals, and no time spent just devoted to the child. Bibles were scarcely brought with the children to the unit … only their clothes and ragged teddy bears. Prayer was rare to hear during family time.

Over the course of this book, God revealed many things to me about who He created me to be and what my purpose is. He has re-charged my passion for helping. During the course of writing this book, He has led me back into doing that very thing. The enemy has attacked me on several occasions and has attempted to fill my heart with fear. God, however, has filled it with His Word and has answered my prayer for protection against fear and evil.

Fear.

It's a powerful weapon the enemy loves to use. Combined with the "what ifs" of life, it can be paralyzing. It can keep us from being all God has called us to be. My fears generally stem around how writing this book could impact others; my family, Christopher's family, the other workers involved that March 4 night. I didn't want to "stir up" anyone's hurt by telling this story. If I thought more harm than good would come from this, I would have stopped telling my story. If I didn't think the Lord was leading me, I would have stopped writing over all these years. I would have stopped sharing my testimony.

I simply would have just *stopped*.

But God hasn't told me to stop. On the contrary, He continues to tell me to go. Daily. He sits on my shoulder and constantly talks to me, reminding me that He is there. Always and forever. So as long as He is faithful to me, I must be faithful to His direction. I'm not going to stop talking or writing simply because I'm afraid. I have to trust His word. "'For I know the plans I have for you,' declares the Lord, 'plans to prosper you and *not to harm you*, plans to give you hope and a future'" (Jeremiah 29:11–12, emphasis added).

I rest in the promise that He knows better than I do how He is going to use the book to touch other peoples' lives; hopefully yours. I prayed so many times that God would lift this burden of fear from my heart, so I could freely share the good - the hope - that has come from the tragedy. He has faithfully answered my prayers and has armed me with only the protection He can provide.

> "Finally, be strong in the Lord and in his might power. Put on the full armor of God so that you can take your stand against the devil's schemes. For our struggle is not against flesh and blood, but against rulers, against the authorities, against the powers of this dark world and against the spiritual forces of evil in the heavenly realms. Therefore put on the full armor of God, so that when the day of evil comes, you may be able to stand your ground, and after you have done everything, to stand. Stand firm then, with the belt of truth buckled around your waist, with the breastplate of righteousness in place, and with your feet fitted with the readiness that comes from the gospel of peace. In addition to all this, take up the shield of faith, with which you can extinguish all the flaming arrows of the evil one. Take the helmet of salvation and the sword of the Spirit, which is the word of God." (Ephesians 6:10–17, NIV).

By lifting the fear up in prayer and by standing behind the "armor of God," I am able to be the warrior He has called me to be. I have put everything I have into this book: my heart, my soul, my tears, and the love I have for the Lord. I have tried my very best to put this passion into words, and now I pray that I can put it back into the *works*.

God has pulled me through so *many* dark days, and He can and will do the same for you.

I want to help God's children; but it doesn't stop there. I want to be one of God's vessels to *help* other people and to heal their souls through the Word of God. I want to be *His* charter girl, someone to help people get from where they are to where He wants them.

He is the only one who has that power … not a new toy, not a Popsicle, and most certainly not a pill. I stated before that over the years many people have asked me, "If you could have done anything different, would you?" For years my answer was always no. Over the course of time, God has shown me I *would* have done things differently. During a recent devotion, God spoke to me through the story from Mark, 9:17–18 (emphasis added): "A man in the crowd answered, 'Teacher, I brought you my son, who is possessed by a spirit that has robbed him of his speech. *Whenever it seizes him, it throws him to the ground.* He foams at the mouth, gnashes his teeth, and becomes rigid. I asked your disciples to drive out the spirit, but they could not.'"

During the dialogue between this man and Jesus, he continues to explain that this evil spirit has plagued him and caused him to seize for many years *from childhood*. Later, Jesus commanded the spirit in verse 25: "you deaf and mute spirit," he said "I command you, come out of him and never enter him again." At that moment, the spirit came out. Later, the disciples spoke to Jesus and said (verse 28) "why couldn't we drive it out?" Jesus replied in verse 29, "This kind can come out only by prayer."

As I read this, an amazing wave of emotion and revelation hit me. I equated the story of this seizing boy to what I saw on March 4. Just like the disciples, those of us involved that night didn't have the power to save Christopher on our strength alone. So, as the old saying goes, "If I knew then, what I know now" … I would have prayed.

"Is any one of you in trouble? He should pray. Is anyone happy? Let him sing songs of praise. Is any one of you sick? He should call the elders of the church to pray over him and anoint him with oil in the name of the Lord" (James 5:13–14, NIV).

The children in the hospital, all of them, needed *more of Him*. We all do. God knows, our communities, our country, our world needs more of Him in hopes of a better future. Jeremiah 15:16 says, "Your words were found, and I ate them, and Your word was to me the joy and rejoicing of my heart." Our world needs God's Word. We need it as we need bread and water. It offers a foundation of faith, a refilling of the soul and a new way to deal with life; a better way.

In fact, the best way.

Many of those children touched my life in ways they will never know. Unfortunately, one of those lives has touched me in a way that I will never be the same. Christopher's death impacted me in so many ways, ways I cannot fully explain through a keyboard or pen and paper.

But just as He used that tragedy to open my eyes, I pray He will open your heart to be receptive to the lessons I have learned. This world is full of difficult things; things we can't truly understand. God created the world and all that's in it. He understands. He is the *only* permanent fix to whatever problem you will ever encounter. You can depend on Him for everything in your life. He offers the greatest love of all through His Son, Jesus Christ. If you know Jesus Christ as your personal savior, then spread His Word. If you don't know Him, please, I am begging, seek Him and get to know Him.

I will *never* forget March 4, 1998. I will forever cherish March 4, 2001. For on that date, the ultimate lifeguard saved me. Jesus is my hero, and I look to Him for everything.

He is my Greatest Love of All.

"Greater love has no one than this, that He lay down his life for his friends" (John 15:13, NIV).

CHAPTER 22

That's Life!

If I had a dollar for every time I heard this when I was growing up ... well, I'd have a lot of dollars. It was one of Dad's favorite expressions! This overused phrase implies that we just have to deal with life as it comes, that there is no real way to navigate through it. It suggests the idea that there is no perfect solution; no perfect way to live. Often, when these words left Dad's mouth, they were accompanied by the tossing up of his palms. Sometimes that's all we can do, *lift up our hands and reach for God,* when life's struggles come at us.

But as a believer in Christ, I know differently now. Life is a series of events. As human beings, we experience triumphs and tribulations. Some come to us as surprises, others are anticipated. We experience wondrous events such as births, graduations, marriages, promotions, and lending a helping hand. These events fill us up, put smiles on our faces, and restore our faith in humanity.

Unfortunately, as easy as that wave of life comes in, it also goes out. We experience difficult moments: divorce, deceit, disloyalty, disease, destruction and death. It often seems like we are never going to survive the bad moments and we can't seem to slow the good times down. We can cause a lot of grief in our own lives through the choices we make. But even in the moments of good choices, the world can still catch us in the wrong place at the wrong time. We are forced to deal with events that don't offer meaning, reason or explanation.

Fortunately, we have a God who sees it all. More importantly, He is *with* us through it all. He stands beside us, behind us, and in front of us. Not only does He walk with us, He has a plan to use each piece of our life puzzle, for His purpose. *Nothing* is wasted. When the pleas of a parent of a wayward teen seem to go unanswered, God is still there. When cancer calls our name, God is still there. When a soldier comes home from war, in a box, God is still there. It may not *feel* like it, but He is still there. His grace, mercy, and love will carry us through those times when we lack the strength to take the next step. *We do not have to take on this world alone.* The Bible is proof of Jesus' work in the midst of storms. And the disciples got a front-row seat to witness His power in their storm. When the disciples' white-knuckled hands clung to the side of the boat while being tossed by the ferocious waves, Jesus was napping in the boat. When the panicking passengers woke him, He wasn't worried. He remained calm. (The kind of calming presence I want when those uninvited life moments happen.) He didn't panic, didn't break a sweat. He looked at the shaking men in the boat and said, *"You of little faith, why are you so afraid?* Then he got up and rebuked the winds and the waves, and it was completely calm"* (Matthew 8:26, NIV, emphasis added). He spoke words and the winds stop.

Simple, huh?

So why do we still doubt? Because doubt comes from the enemy.

Many times during my journey I have listened to preachers talk about "the enemy." So what does the enemy look or feel like? Helpless, hopeless, frustrated, worried, scared, depressed? All of the above. This is the enemy at work on our soul. The enemy doesn't like us to be empowered by God because it decreases his power. The enemy knows that if he can play games with our minds, we will begin to question God's promise. And that's where the quicksand of worry and hopelessness suck us down and destruction plants a seed.

Our lack of hope occurs during the rough times when we lack faith in Him. That's why His word is so crucial to our faith. His promises of steadfast love permeate the Bible. John 2:28 says, "And now, dear children, continue in Him, so that when He appears we may be confident and unashamed before Him at His coming." God wants us to hold on to Him with all of our might … and He promises not to let go of the rope, ever. Continue in Him.

In moments of uncertain and horrifying circumstances, it's natural to question "why?" But posing that question is different than doubt. Doubt questions trust and ability. "Why" seeks reason and explanation. But when you ask that question, don't expect an instant-message answer. If you do get the answer on this side of Heaven, it usually evolves and reveals itself through time and a lot of patience. It rarely appears overnight. And, there will be some circumstances in life that even on the other side of Heaven, we still do not understand. But my belief in God and the promises of His Word tell me that despite the circumstances, *there is always hope.* And there is so much comfort in that truth. I rest in that. I rest in knowing that I know the One who provides that hope. And through the process of getting to know Him, He taught me this: there is purpose in our pain and suffering. Romans 5:3–4 states, "Not only so, but we also rejoice in our sufferings, because we know that suffering produces perseverance; perseverance, character, and character, hope." Trust that there is a lesson. Allow that struggle to deepen your dependency on Him and to foster your faith in Him. Continue in Him, stepping forward and persevering through His strength. And that is the hope and blessing that comes when we learn to depend on Him. But it all starts by making a decision, a choice.

Choice. Think about it. Every day you wake up, breathe, think, make decisions, and act upon those decisions. Before we even get to the office, gym, or school, we have already decided what to wear, what to eat for breakfast, and how to act in each of our environments. We have decided to either buy or take our lunch that day, and we've decided whether to drive our car, take the bus, or walk. All these decisions require thought and planning, even though we often don't acknowledge these decisions taking place.

We experience the outcome of our choices, sometimes without

even realizing we have chosen them. Thinking, deciding, and acting all require work, whether it's a conscious effort or not. One of the greatest and potentially detrimental choices we make is who we chose to follow and love. We can choose to love Him, or we can choose to love ourselves. When we love ourselves more than God, we find ourselves centered on stuff: things, money, activities, and sin.

Is God involved in your choices? How *often* do you involve Him? Wednesday night? Sunday morning? When the preacher says, "Let us pray"? But what about the times in between? When we are alone in our thoughts? Or staring at the computer screen at work? Or watching the driver in front of us hit the brakes in bumper-to-bumper traffic? Does God wait for us to slow down and come to Him? Do we make time for Him every day?

As humans, we think we have all the answers and know what is best for us, and we make choices based upon our limited knowledge. That, combined with the free will God gives us, can foster a false sense of security that leads us into the belief that we don't need to consult Him. More often than not, we leave Him out of those choices and then wonder how our lives have gone astray and we are faced with so many problems.

But God knows better. He *always* knows better.

God knows our thoughts before we think them. He knows when we hurt, though we carry a smile on our face to get through the day. And He knows His plan for our lives. "Before I formed you in the womb I knew you, before you were born I set you apart" (Jeremiah 1:5, NIV). Did you get that? He knew us even *before* our parents knew they are pregnant! God is in the know, all the time. Not only does God know us, as individuals, He knows the plans for our lives. Jeremiah 29:11 says, "For I know the plans I have for you, the plans to prosper and not harm." Do you believe Him at His Word? Do you have faith in Him?

Faith. That's a big word, one that I have struggled with, to be honest. Growing up in the public school system, we are taught that a fact is only something that can be proven. But thank God, He is not limited by that rule. Just because we can't see it, smell it, or hear it doesn't mean it doesn't exist. Faith is a difficult thing for some—we can't see it, touch it or smell it. We can only trust and believe it exists. This, my friend, involves choice.

God offers this comfort: "I tell you the truth, if you have faith as small *as a mustard seed*, you can say to this mountain, 'Move from here to there' and it will move. *Nothing* will be impossible for you" (Matthew 17:20, NIV, emphasis added). A mustard seed. Really? Do you know how small a mustard seed is? And if I have that much faith in God, I can tell a mountain to move? Wow! Hard to believe? It was for me too. That's why it's a choice. You either believe it or you don't.

Please choose to believe it.

My trial was the catalyst in my life that prompted me to ask the question, who do I put my faith in? I wrestled with this for a long time and went 'round and 'round with the "why" question. I exhausted myself; I became defeated and deflated. Maybe you can relate. But here's the awesome news: we don't have to stay there! Just as our grammar school teacher taught us, there are four Ws: Why? Who? What? Where? So don't forget to ask about the other three.

God, His Word, His Promises everywhere = His plan.

And *that's life* with God.

"Come, let us go up to the mountain of the LORD, to the temple of the God of Jacob. He will teach us His ways, so that we may walk in His path" (Micah 4:2, NIV).

CHAPTER 23

There Is Purpose in Pain

Praise God for pain! Yep. That's right. I thank Him for choosing me. To be the one accused. To be the one to stand trial. Can't believe I'm writing that? Here's why I'm thankful. Without this suffering, I probably would not have recognized my need for a Savior. I would not have turned to Him. I would not be the person I am today. I would not be where I am today, standing firm on faith.

I would not be a follower of Christ.

I know now that He had a purpose for my pain. I just didn't understand it at that time. And I certainly didn't like it. But I am changed from it. When I wanted to crumble and slip into a hole, He gave me the strength to stand. He made me stand up for what I believe in. When I wanted to take a step back into depression, He made me push forward. When I wanted to roll over and keep my head under the covers, He made me get out of bed. He made me persevere.

You know the old saying, "What doesn't kill you makes you stronger"? Well, it won't. Not without God. God will make you stronger. Many times, during my poor-me moments, I wanted a one-way ticket out of this world. God wouldn't let me. He had a better solution for my pain. And it's spelled, H-O-P-E. Healing, Opportunity, Purpose, Eternally. He gave me a one-way ticket— only His ticket goes to heaven. I have hope. I know anywhere I go in life, He stands before me. He holds me in His hand and keeps me humble. He forgives me when I am unforgivable. He loves me when I am unlovable. He accepts me when I am unacceptable.

"If it's not broken, don't fix it." Well, God allowed brokenness in me. That's the only way He could fix me. I know that concept is difficult to comprehend. Dr. Charles Stanley articulates this point better than I can in his book, *The Blessings of Brokenness*. Listen to this. He writes,

> God does not allow brokenness in our lives because he is ruthless, cruel, heartless, or without compassion. No! To the contrary. God sees the full potential for our lives, and he deeply desires an intimate, loving spiritual relationship with us. He wants to bring about our best, and for us to experience him in the fullness of his love, wisdom, power, strength, and goodness. He allows brokenness in our lives *in order to bring about* a blessing. (Stanley, 1997).

That's the only reason I have found for the "why" question. The trial put me in a place that I, alone, was unable to recover from. It made me dependent and broken. It made me uncomfortable. It made me realize I had very little control over my life. Though I knew I had done nothing wrong in that hospital on that March night, I still needed help. I was lost in the world, desperately searching for healing, strength, purpose and love.

My needs went deep because the hurt was deep. The trial made me question everything about my life. I questioned my existence. I questioned my purpose. I questioned my future. I questioned *everything* and *everyone*. I needed guidance. I needed assurance. I needed to know that there was a light at the end of a very long, dark, and scary tunnel. And, most of all, I needed forgiveness from my sins. God gave me His forgiveness. I just had to *accept* His grace and mercy.

God met all these needs and many more; *that's the blessing* that comes after being broken. He gave me the resources I needed to survive and persevere. Many of these resources came in human form: family, attorneys, and friends. They offered comfort through words, hugs, phone calls, prayers, and encouragement. "You have so many people pulling for you and praying for you. You'll never know how many people are with you," David said so many times. Family members told me, "It will be okay." They tried to reassure me I did nothing wrong. But still something was missing. I wanted to *know* I would be okay. I wanted to *know* the jury would believe I did nothing wrong. I wanted assurance, and no one, not even my knowledgeable attorneys, could assure me with 100 percent confidence.

"You are not alone," David said more than once. He was right. I wasn't alone. I just didn't realize how non-alone I really was. I had the biggest, boldest, best-equipped counselor with me all the way. I had to trust and believe in something higher. I had to have faith. And once I believed Him, I had hope.

It has now been more than fifteen years since this tragic event. My life has not been easy … extremely trying at times. Though through each new trial, I have a reference point. I remember the hurt, the disappointment, and the emptiness I experienced as a result of the death and the trial. I tried, unsuccessfully, to fill that hole with many things, but the only One that truly refills my spirit is the Lord. When I turn to Him and say, "I can't do this," He always gives me strength to face one more day. Our trials are not without purpose.

1 Peter 1:6–9 says, "In this time you greatly rejoice, though now for a little while you may have had to suffer grief in all kinds of trials. These have come so that your faith of greater worth than gold, which perishes even though refined by fire may be proved genuine and may result in praise, glory, and honor when Jesus Christ is revealed."

He has promised each of us that His plans for our lives are distinct and purposeful. It is our responsibility to take the walk with Him, trusting and leaning on Him to lead us through the adversities, and yes, even to thank Him for the trials. For in the trials we find out who we really are, what we really believe, who we trust, and where we put our faith. Through our trials, God gives us the answers to the other three Ws.

And that, my friend, is purpose.

"Not only so, but we also rejoice in our sufferings, because we know that suffering produces perseverance; perseverance, character; and character, hope" (Romans 5:3-4, NIV).

CHAPTER 24

His Work on the Cross

On this side of Heaven, we are guaranteed to experience dissatisfaction. We live in a world of wanting more. More money, faster cars, bigger houses; the list goes on and on. When we don't get what we want, we are dissatisfied. Dissatisfaction leads to emotional instability, control issues, and sin. If we build our foundation on anything or anyone other than God, we need to rebuild. If our foundation is God, we can truly let go of our burdens and insecurities and *know* God has complete control, even in the darkest times. He hears our cries for help, guidance, and clarity. He answers our prayers … on His watch. And just as parents nurture and direct their children's steps, God directs the steps of His children.

Most of us have heard of the twelve-step program for those who are addicted to alcohol, food, sex, drugs, or other substances. The first step involves acceptance of the addiction, admitting we are powerless and in need of help. Many struggle with this aspect, admitting, owning, or embracing their weakness, and it limits them from moving forward toward healing and restoration. The process can continue for months, years, and sometimes a lifetime.

As does our walk with the Lord.

We experience moments of elation and moments of isolation. The highs and lows make us feel like we live our life in a boat that is easily tossed by the waves of the world. Jesus knows when those storms will hit, and He is right by our side in the boat. How we respond to the storm solely depends on our focus. If our focal point rests on the waves, we will live on the roller-coaster ride of worry, aimless wandering, and wasting time and energy. But if we fix our eyes on Jesus, we can rest in His security rather than the volatility of the circumstances.

I know this through experience. I rode those waves for a long time. But I'm not stuck there anymore. When I find myself wanting answers to life's question, I now seek Heaven's direction. That's what keeps me moving forward, keeps me focused.

It all goes back to where our focus is.

Christ.

God sent His son to this Earth for a one specific reason—to pay the admission ticket for us, for you, to cross Heaven's threshold (Romans 6:23). Without His work, we were guaranteed to spend eternity in misery; misery beyond what we can even comprehend. That gift had a price tag larger than any bank account on this planet.

Simply said, you can't pay it back. And the truth of God's

grace is He doesn't expect us to. He just asks you to *receive it* and then tell others about His work in your life. That, my dear reader, is the reason you are holding this book in your hands.

Every day I am reminded of where I was, and I am humbled beyond words for where I am now. And it's all because of the cross. That doesn't mean life now is all a big field of daises. Naturally I still experience times of sadness. However, instead of allowing that sadness to snowball into a pit of despair, I now ask my Heavenly Father to carry me through those moments, and He always lightens my load. "Come to me, all you who are weary and burdened, and I will give you rest. Take my yoke upon you and learn from me, for I am gentle and humble in heart, and you will find rest for your souls. For my yoke is easy and my burden is light" (Matthew 11:28–30, NIV).

In my wildest and craziest dreams, I never would have imagined that the hand of "life cards" I was dealt would lead me to this point in my life. Only when I got to the place of true surrender did I begin to experience peace. I still have to make choices in my life, but now I turn to God for guidance. And He has steadfastly guided me here, to accept Him, to trust Him, to follow Him.

To tell you this story.

In fact, it is only because of many prayers, pleas to Heaven's throne, that this book even exists. I have repeatedly asked God to show me His will. And every time, I hear the voice of His Angels: "Follow Him". When initially given that instruction, I was worried, rather terrified, that I will be "on trial" again, given the nature of the emotions and life changes experienced by everyone involved that March night. However, I trust in God's promises of protection that the courtroom-drama part of this story is over. I *know* that's not the focus He intended for this book. It's so painful to recount. And God doesn't stir up hurt, for the sake of inflicting more pain. The focus of this book is about the work on the cross, to restore, redeem and provide true healing.

Thank You for Your work on the cross, Jesus.

CHAPTER 25

The New You

So what does all of this have to do with you? Hopefully my story has influenced your life in some way to change your thoughts and behaviors, to rewire the way your brain thinks and responds to circumstances and struggles. One of my prayers for you is that as you read my story, you may apply the lessons to your life. You can start by paying closer attention in your own life: to the people God puts in your path, to the signs that are staring you in the face. I pray that God uses this book to prick your heart, to see the glimpse of His light in the forest of life that seems so dark, to embrace the light and allow it to guide your life.

Maybe He's been working on your heart, and reading my story has just given you that final push to say "yes" to God. Say "yes" to His plan, not yours. "Yes" to a life that is focused on important things like your family, their souls, their passions, purpose, dreams and, more importantly, their eternal destiny. Or maybe this book is a starting point. Maybe you don't know

Christ. Do you feel embarrassed by that? That's okay. I did too. Guess what? That's how every one of us started out.

Not knowing.

Maybe you are like I used to be: cynical, sarcastic, impatient, and stubborn (okay, I still have my moments with the last two). Or maybe you are just at a place in your life that feels like the bottom of a muddy, smelly pond. You can't see the sun trying to shine through all the muck. You can't hear God's call on your life because there is too much "mud of the world" in your ears. For any of these scenarios—here's the Good News—God doesn't judge you about where you are or where you have been. He cares about where you are going. That's what the cross was all about—your eternal life. Forgiveness of your sin. His work on the cross is a gift, and gifts are intended to have recipients. "For it is by grace you have been saved, through faith—and this is not from yourselves, it is the *gift* of God" (Ephesians 2:8, NIV, emphasis added).

Have you received this gift yet?

If not, what are you waiting for?

Life with Christ is so much better than life without Him. We can have fun without Him, but we can have *more* fun with Him. I know. I've had both. His fun is better, though, because it doesn't require us to give up our purity, our conscience, or our morals. We can have the blessing of Him right now, wherever we are, even in the circus of life.

I recently took my kids to the circus. I've always loved the circus. The animals are so beautiful and well-trained. The clowns offer a few good chuckles, and the costumes are vibrant and colorful. And all of the participants are so talented! From the acrobats to the lion tamers to the tightrope walker! Of all of the acts, my favorite part has always been watching the trapeze artists. They "fly through the air with the greatest of ease," hanging onto a bar, swinging back and forth, letting go, and catching their partner's hand. It's awesome! And I think I like it more than other acts because they always have a net under them to catch them if they fall. *It takes away so much fear knowing they have that security.*

Just a week following the circus, I was reading a chapter in a book called *Jesus, Life Coach.* (Jones, 2006) The particular topic I read was on "productivity." The author, Laurie Beth Jones, wrote about how when we say yes to God, He smiles and leads us into His plan. It also mentioned—and *don't miss this part*—that sometimes our walk with God is a lot like a trapeze act. Jesus is hanging from the swing, arms stretched out waiting to catch us and move us to a new place … and many times we just hold on to our spiritual swing and don't trust Him not to let us fall. We seem to forget His safety net *won't let* us fall, and we hold on to what is safe. And we miss out on all the fun He has for us. We miss the opportunities that He has and we miss the blessings.

This devotion, following on the heels of our trip to the circus, really hit me like a frying pan upside my highlighted head. So many times I am that person hanging onto my own swing, afraid to let go and trust that God is not going to let me fall. And even if I do fall, Jesus is the net that lay below me. He is the greatest guarantee we have. His Word promises, "I will never leave you nor forsake you" (Hebrews 13:5, NIV).

He. Will. Never. Leave. *You.*

Trust Him!

CHAPTER 26

Your Elevator Speech

Our daughter has a carbon copy of my sleep pattern; she likes to sleep, a lot. We both would prefer to stay in bed most of the morning, snuggled under our favorite blankets, in our cozy pajamas until the demands of our tummies prompted us to get up. We think the bears have the right idea about sleep: hibernation. However, the obligation to be on time for school and work doesn't afford either of us a chance to keep snoozing during the week.

On a particular fall Monday morning, when the air was crisp and cool, I peeled myself out of bed and went up to her room to wake her for school. As she lay in the bed, surrounded by dozens of her stuffed animals, blankets, and pillows, she rolled over, opened her eyes, and exclaimed, "I hate Mondays!"

Though I shared that feeling, I held back my smile and softly whispered these words to myself: *Amen, Baby Doll, Amen.*

After the crazy morning madness of getting dressed, packing lunches, eating a bit of breakfast, brushing teeth, and dropping the kids off at school, I headed to work. I parked the car in the city parking deck across the street from my office and stepped onto the elevator. Standing there, with a smile consuming her face, was a young woman I knew. In my sarcastic tone, much like my daughter's attitude, I said to her, "Yeah. It's Monday." She offered a gentle smile and said, "I love Mondays. I love all days. They are all a gift from God."

Ouch.

I was quickly put in my place. Her comment was not delivered in an offensive or rude manner; much to the contrary. She was genuine in her speech. I know this because I know her. She is a devote Christian; the kind I look up to. She walks the walk and obviously, talks the talk. My toes were becoming black and blue because the conviction of the Holy Spirit stepped on them. She had an attitude of gratitude. And I was a disgruntled, cranky, tired mess. My attitude was swayed based on how I felt rather than what it should stand on—God's grace for giving me new day.

Ironically, a few weeks later, on a Friday afternoon, I left my office and headed out the door, excited for the weekend. I crossed the street, walked into the parking deck, and hopped onto the elevator. This time, an older gentleman and I had a brief conversation. "Hello. How are you?" I asked.

He responded, "Well, it will depend on what the judge says next week." Obviously, he had spent his day in court and was anxious about a pending legal matter. Much like my grouchy Monday-morning elevator speech, it was clear his attitude was dependent upon his circumstances. Now, to be fair, I didn't know that man. I don't know what life circumstances he faced. I don't know what his beliefs were. I don't know if he stands on any foundation of faith. I did not judge him but reflected on the lesson I had been taught just a few weeks prior.

Having an attitude of gratitude, even in the difficult days of life, is what *should* set us apart from those who do not know the Lord, or the joy that comes by walking with the Lord through life. That, in and of itself, is cause for a positive perspective in life. And that positivity is what our praise to the Lord is all about. "Come, let us sing for joy to the LORD; let us shout aloud to the rock of our salvation. Let us come before Him with thanksgiving and extol Him with music and song" (Psalm 95:1–2, NIV).

When I first read that Scripture, I thought, *Oh boy, I'm in trouble. I can't carry a tune in a bucket.* I'm not a singer, or at least not a good one. But that's not what the message is portraying. Everything we do, we should do with an attitude of praise. Speaking, writing, singing, working, playing, folding clothes, washing dishes, changing diapers, mowing the grass—*everything*.

That's what worship is.

Over the past few weeks, a large focus in our couples' class in church has been about this very topic: how we praise, worship, share, show, and have an attitude of gratitude for what Christ has done in our life. Now, our class knows I am as extroverted as they come; I could talk for hours, in our class, about what Christ has done in my life. Those who know Him understand the walk of a Christian; those are the comfortable conversations. But as we have discussed in our class, the struggle I and many other Christians have in common is the fear or hesitation in talking about what Christ has done, outside the walls of a church. And really, that's what Christ calls us to do. "Therefore go and make disciples of all nations, baptizing them in the name of the Father and of the Son and of the Holy Spirit" (Matthew 29:18, NIV). Our praise and worship should extend beyond the rows of pews in church.

That is where the road meets the rubber. That is why you are reading this book.

"Let the peace of Christ rule in your hearts, since as members of one body you were called to peace. *And be thankful.* Let the message of Christ dwell among you richly as you teach and admonish one another with all wisdom through psalms, hymns, and songs from the Spirit, singing to God with *gratitude in your hearts.* And whatever you do, whether in word or deed, do it all in the name of the Lord Jesus, *giving thanks* to God the Father through him" (Colossians 3:15–17, NIV, emphasis added).

So let me ask you. Knowing what you know about Christ, about the work of the cross, about the forgiveness of your sins, about redemption from your past, about restoration with your Heavenly Father, what will be your elevator speech?

CHAPTER 27

My Father's Wisdom

Code 1, for Christ's sake!

Consider this book an intervention. A spiritual, psychological, and emotional intervention on behalf of Jesus Christ. For you. You just read this book for a reason. Don't dismiss it! Pay attention to what God is speaking to you *right now*. Something in this book, in this story, is what He wanted you to hear. This book was placed in your hands for a reason. If you picked it up off the shelf, there was a reason. If a friend gave it to you as a gift, there was a reason. If you get nothing out of my story but gained everything from hearing how God has worked, for His glory, in my life, there is a reason.

That reason?

Because He can and will do the same for you.

Have you allowed Him that chance? Have you allowed Him into your heart? Have you put down your fears, pains, hurts, and grudges to allow Him to wrap His loving arms around you? He wants to. He tells us so in His Word. Did you know that? I didn't either—not then. But I do now. He wants to know you too. His Word tells me so.

My father was a smart man. But his knowledge didn't reach the depths of the endless wisdom that is offered through God's Word. My dad wasn't completely correct in his teachings.

"Nobody's perfect," he said. Yes, there *is* a perfect man. His name is Jesus. He is the perfect physician. He can heal anyone if they bring their hurt to Him. He is the perfect counselor. He knows, better than any, what you need to hear. And He wants to meet that need and many, many more. Things you don't even know you need. He is the perfect teacher. He wrote an entire book. It's called the Bible. You'll never need to read another book once you've read His.

"Do your best," Dad would cheer. Sometimes our best still isn't good enough, so we have to rely on God's strength. "I can do all things through Christ who strengthens me" (Philippians 4:13).

I could not have survived Dad's death on my own. I could not have survived the trial on my own. Both times I wanted a one-way ticket out of this world. God gave me that. God's grace, mercy, and strength were the only tools that pulled me out of the depths of hurt and self-pity. And now they are the only strengths that are enabling me to be courageous enough to write this book and to "stand up and tell you what I believe in."

I believe in Jesus Christ. "Stand up and say to them whatever I command you. Do not be terrified by them, or I will terrify you before them" (Jeremiah 1:17, NIV). I wanted to tell the world what God has done in my life … who the real Meg is and who she has become. I am a child of the One and Only. I am a child of God. And now, I'm His follower. There is no one like Him. He is now and will be forever my first true love. I am an advocate for Jesus Christ. I want others to learn about Him. I want them to accept Him. I want you to know Him, intimately, like I do. I want them (you) to realize *you are not alone.* You don't have to face *one more second* alone. He is sitting right beside you as you read. Do you feel His presence?

"Life's not fair." Nope, it's not. Dad was right about this one. This world is not fair. A child battling cancer is not fair. A fourteen-year-old boy hooked on heroin, is not fair. A woman beaten by her husband but too afraid to leave, is not fair. Seven years of remission from colon cancer, only to be told, "It's back," is not fair. Losing your job after twenty-four years of loyal service to a company, is not fair. Foreclosure on your house is not fair.

But there is justice.

God holds the key to justice. Let Him go before you; let Him handle your burdens. He knows every intention of every person. You can't fool Him. He's already got you pegged. Stop running from Him. Don't waste any more time in your pit of self-defeating behavior.

It's not worth the cost.

He's there, with open arms, to hold you when you just can't bear to take the next step along the path in life. He wants to be your Source for everything. He wants to show you just how far He can take you. The very thing that has you down will be the very thing *He* uses to build you up. And when I say up, I mean *up*. Higher than the tops of the mountains overlooking the valleys you've been in. You'll be so high you'll struggle to catch your breath. Clean, crisp, fresh, *Godly* air. There's no drug in this world that will give you a better buzz, one the angels will hear in heaven. They'll actually want to come down to see what the party is all about.

It's invigorating to watch Him work. It's exhilarating to know you are loved *that much*, and not because of anything you do. Too good to be true? I dare you to find out for yourself. I dare you to submit yourself to Him and allow Him to fulfill those dreams He has given you.

Dreams. We all have them. Some while we slumber, some while we slump over a computer during the daylight hours. But I'm talking about the dreams that live in our core. The dreams that stir us, that foster that lump in our throats. That thing that's on our bucket list that just won't stop asking the question, "When are you going to pursue me?"

I believe each person on this Earth was put here for specific purposes and given a combination of skills, knowledge, experiences—these are all gifts. Though we may share similar aspects, humans are unique from one another due to the *combination* of these aspects and our life experiences. That combination gives us our individuality; that individuality comes from our Creator. He carefully and craft-fully designed each and every one of us. He even knows the "number of hairs on our head" (Matthew 10:30, NIV). He knows us intimately: how we feel, what we think, what we are passionate about, what makes us tick. But He even takes us a step further. He didn't just form us, bring us into the world, and let us go. He loves us so much, He has taken the time to write the plan for our lives. Your book. My book. His book. Her book.

And what does He say about those God-given desires? "Delight yourself also in the Lord, and He will give you the desires of your heart" (Psalm 37:4, NIV).

Don't believe it? Listen to this. As a young girl I always dreamed, more than anything, of being a wife and mommy. A boy and a girl, please. I dreamed of helping others. I dreamed I would be a counselor assisting people in finding their passions and, more importantly, helping them put a plan in place to pursue those passions. I almost let March 4 steal those from me. I thought I would never find a spouse who would understand the trials of my past. *And then I married Dale.* After seven months of trying to conceive, I was convinced I was being punished and would never have any children. *And then the pregnancy test was positive.* We were having *a boy.* And four years later, *a girl.* I tried to turn my back on the world of helping. Believe me, I tried. But the dreams God puts inside of us are undeniable.

It's what He made us for.

The desires God gives are the admission tickets to our calling. He welcomes us to pursue those things that make us stop and stare in awe of other's circumstances and compels us to do something. The firefighter who *is compelled to* run into that burning building. The soldier who *wants* to go back for a second tour of duty. The teacher who accepts a pitiful paycheck because she *delights in* watching her students learn.

As for me, my days of swinging a hammer are still alive. I like to build bridges. Not physical ones, though. I love helping others construct a connection from where they are to where God wants to take them. I thrive on helping people discover how their heaven-appointed talents, gifts, abilities, and passions intersect to fulfill their God-given purpose. I get teary-eyed watching the three-year-old boy's eyes light up as he lies on the floor, watching the wheels on the toy train turn, asking the question, "How does that work?" I am a cheerleader for the teenager who tells her mom and dad, "I want to be a missionary in China." When the forty-five-year-old man crosses the stage to accept his long-awaited medical degree following years of misery in corporate America, my heart skips a beat.

Passion.

Vision.

Dreams.

Purpose.

We all have them. What's yours?

Oh, and as for my dream of becoming a counselor ... I crossed the stage in May.

To God be the Glory.

"And we know that in all things God works for the good of those who love Him, who have been called according to His purpose" (Romans 8:28, NIV).

Acknowledgments

To Mom: Thank you for loving me, teaching me, believing in me, and standing beside me throughout my life and especially during my trial. Despite the heartaches, I have learned so many great things from you and Dad. I really wouldn't change a thing. I love you, Mom!

To Dad: I miss you so much. As I look back on the time I had with you, I am thankful. Though there were difficult days, and few too many, I cherish those moments, the conversations, and the relationship we had. I love you and pray that whenever my time comes to step through the gates of heaven, you are standing there to greet me.

To Jason: Thanks, bro! We've stood beside each other through a lot in our lives. Thank you for believing in me and being strong when I was so weak. I am honored to be called your sister, and I am so proud of you. Thank you for being who you are and for serving our country. I love you!

To Dale: Thank you for allowing me to share my journey with you without judgment. Thank you for loving me. Thank you for asking me to be your wife and step-mom to the boys. Thank you for encouraging me to "keep writing." Thank you for our children. You know how much I love and adore being a mother to them. I love you so much!

To Charlie and Parks: Thank you for accepting me. Thank you for loving me as a mom. I love you both and pray you live your lives in accordance to God's plan and purpose.

To Ayden and Molly: You bring so much joy to my life! I love being your Mommy, and I hope and pray that one day, you will experience the same joys of being a parent to your own children. I pray for your hearts, that you know, accept, and love Jesus as your Savior. Always know that God loves you and accepts you as you are, just as Daddy and I love, accept, and believe in you. You are my angels. I love you!

To David: Thank you for all your wisdom, knowledge, strength, and comforting words during my trial. I cherish our friendship now and hope and pray God continues to use you to help others just as you helped me through one of the darkest moments of my life. And, of course, thanks for all the tissues.

To Locke: Thank you for all of the wisdom, energy, and lightheartedness. You managed to offer comic relief when nothing about my trial was funny. I appreciate all you did to help me then and I cherish your friendship now.

To Chris: Thank you, girl! I appreciate your help with the trial and all the hours of sleep that you lost and tears you shed on my behalf. I am also grateful for your help with this book—I can't believe it's finally published. God *never* ceases to amaze me!

To My Lord and Savior: "Thank You" is inadequate. You are my rock, my Savior, and my Source for everything. I will continue to tell this story, to bring You the glory and honor You deserve! You are the light in my world, and I will live to give You praise!

References

Afanasieff, Morris, Mccary, Morris, Carey, & Stockman (Composers). (1990). "One Sweet Day." Carey, M., Performer. United States of America.

Colin, C., Monahan, P., Stafford, J., & Underwood, S. (Composers). (2003). "Calling All Angels." Train, Performer. United States of America.

Creed, L. and M. Masser (Composer). (1977). "The Greatest Love of All." G. Benson, Original Performer; W. Houston, Performer. United States of America.

Ferch, S. R. "Intentional Forgiving as a Counseling Intervention." *Journal of counseling and development (76)* (1998), 261–70.

Fuller, M. *The Theology of the Hammer.* Smyth & Helwys Publishing, Inc. (1994).

Jones, L. B. *Jesus Life Coach: Learn from the Best.* Thomas Nelson Publishing (2006).

Moore, B. *Living Proof with Beth Moore.* Retrieved October 10, 2012, from http://www.lproof.org/

Neimark, N. M. *Mind/Body Education Center.* Retrieved October

10, 2012, from http://www.thebodysoulconnection.com/EducationCenter/fight.html

Schiltz, D. (Composer). (1978). The Gambler. K. Rogers, Performer. United States of America.

Stanley, C.F. *The Blessings of Brokenness:Why God Allows Us To Go Through Hard Times.* Grand Rapids, MI: Zondervan Publishing House (1997).

Wilson, S. D. *Hurt People Hurt People.* Grand Rapids, MI: Discovery House Publishers (2001).

About the Author

Meg Jordan is a wife, mom, step-mom, Christian counselor and life coach. She enjoys writing and speaking about her life experiences in an effort to share the hope only found in Christ. Her passion lies in being a "bridge builder"; helping people build a bridge from where they are, to where Christ wants them to be. Visit her online at www.megjordanonline.com

CPSIA information can be obtained at www.ICGtesting.com
Printed in the USA
BVOW081643150213

313405BV00001B/15/P